Julia Child Rules

✤

By the Same Author

FICTION
Motherhood Made a Man Out of Me
The Diamond Lane
Trespassers Welcome Here

NONFICTION
How Georgia Became O'Keeffe: Lessons on the Art of Living
The Gospel According to Coco Chanel: Life Lessons from the World's Most Elegant Woman
How to Hepburn: Lessons on Living from Kate the Great
The Stuff of Life: A Daughter's Memoir
Generation Ex: Tales from the Second Wives Club
Big Girl in the Middle (coauthor, with Gabrielle Reece)

FOR YOUNG ADULTS
Minerva Clark Gets a Clue
Minerva Clark Goes to the Dogs
Minerva Clark Gives Up the Ghost

Julia Child Rules

Lessons on Savoring Life

❧

KAREN KARBO

Guilford, Connecticut
An imprint of Globe Pequot Press

skirt!® is an attitude . . . spirited, independent, outspoken, serious, playful and irreverent, sometimes controversial, always passionate.

Text design: Sheryl P. Kober
Project editor: Meredith Dias
Layout: Maggie Peterson

Library of Congress Cataloging-in-Publication Data is available on file.

ISBN 978-0-7627-8309-0

Printed in the United States of America

10 9 8 7 6 5 4 3 2 1

To home cooks everywhere,
and to the memory of my mother, Joan Karbo

It is impossible to be a great chef unless you have a very large soul.

—RUTH REICHL

Save the liver!

—DAN AYKROYD

Contents

RULE ^{No.} 1:

LIVE WITH ABANDON

Life itself is the proper binge.

IN THE SUMMER OF 1946, JULIA MCWILLIAMS AND PAUL CHILD drove across America. A bottle of vodka and a thermos of mixed martinis rolled around the backseat of Julia's Buick. It was a time before air-conditioned vehicles and open-container laws. It was a full year before Jack Kerouac and Neal Cassady went on the road. It was ten years before the passage of the Federal-Aid Highway Act prompted the government to build a decent interstate highway system connecting sea to shining sea. It was twenty-five years before my dad, in a rare chatty moment, offered me this piece of excellent advice: Never marry someone until you've driven cross-country with him in a car without a radio.

Paul and Julia apparently held the same belief, for that's what this trip was all about: getting the full measure of each other without any interruptions. They'd spent two years together

1

working for the OSS, the Office of Strategic Services, during World War II, and now they needed to see if they could stop being coworkers and start being lovers.

They'd met in Ceylon (now Sri Lanka). Resort-like Kandy, set amid emerald-green hills and tea plantations on a balmy sub-tropical plateau, was possibly the most peaceful place in Asia. The environment resembled an ongoing fraternity mixer, if the fraternity was comprised of scholars, anthropologists, sociologists, military strategists, and cartographers, every weekend a flurry of cocktail parties, dinners, cocktail parties, outings, cocktail parties, sightseeing, and cocktail parties. Even though they were both single and the setting was ripe for romance, Julia and Paul just weren't that into each other. There are opposites, and then there are opposites in a parallel universe.

Julia was a strapping California "hayseed," her favorite self-descriptor, a freckle-faced redheaded party girl and prankster whose personal motto at Smith College had been Less Learning, More Moonshine. The only time she felt inspired to improve her mediocre grades was when she learned that seniors who maintained a B average could keep a car on campus.* Her taste in men ran toward "he-men," tall, broad-shouldered guys who were manly in an obvious, golf-playing, hail-fellow-well-met, Southern California Republican sort of way. Paul Child was not this guy. He was too old (forty-two to her thirty-two),

---

* Julia improved her GPA and purchased a 1929 Ford, which she named Eulalie. She used it almost exclusively to venture to speakeasies in nearby Holyoke. The car was a convertible. Most convenient, as it allowed Julia and her friends to get sick over the side without ruining the upholstery.

too short (five foot nine to her six foot three), and not much of a golfer.

Paul was a different kettle of fish: complicated, sophisticated, a painter and photographer, a lover of food and wine, who preferred his women small, dark, brilliant, complicated, and sophisticated.* He found Julia girlish, immature, excitable-verging-on-hysterical. Privately, which is to say in letters to Charlie, his identical twin, he disparaged her awkward virginal quality. Paul was a veteran of numerous love affairs, flings, and dalliances. Before joining the OSS he'd shacked up for years with Edith Kennedy, an erudite woman twenty years his senior. In matters of amour, Paul Child was as French as it was possible for an American man to be.

Paul and Julia headed north and east: San Francisco; Crescent City; Bend, Oregon; Spokane; Coeur d'Alene; Billings; Flint, Michigan; tucking into Canada for a few days; Rochester, New York; then finally, after nearly a month, Lopaus Point, Maine, where Charlie and his wife, Freddie, had a cabin overlooking the Atlantic.

They stayed at crummy motor courts with thin mattresses and thinner walls, slurped down phlegmy eggs at roadside cafes, lingered at dive bars, where Julia plopped herself down on the stool and knocked back whiskey with the locals, who gaped. How tall is that woman anyway? No matter. She was used to it. People had been staring at her for her entire life. When Julia wasn't behind

---

* Paul Child was possibly the last man in America to utter the words "I like my women to be intellectual."

the wheel, she stuck her long legs out the passenger-side window, her toenails painted loose-woman red. She was a thirtysomething spinster at a time when the median age of marriage for women in America was twenty-one.

Before the trip, Paul worried in letters to Charlie that Julia would be prudish and alarmed by the demands of desire. But Julia was a big woman of even bigger appetites. As she would admit in a letter to her friend Avis DeVoto several years later, "Before marriage I was wildly interested in sex." Yes. Julia. *Wildly interested in sex.*

To think of the two of them pulling up to some lonesome high-desert motel (cue the tumbleweeds) in the big Buick, Julia hanging on Paul's shoulder, giggling, barefoot, while Paul secured their room key from the suspicious clerk who scowled as he got a whiff of their martini-infused breath and rocketing hormones, is to get a glimpse of her rebellious spirit, her complete lack of regard for anything resembling conventional behavior or, God forbid, *rules.* She despised rules, and her lifelong way of dealing with them was, in any given situation, to neglect to know them. A simple, elegant solution.

Charlie and Freddie's one-room cabin at Lopaus Point sat at the end of a rutted sandy path, and when Julia and Paul arrived, they had to park the Buick in town and drag their suitcases through the dense woods to get there. Even though it was high summer, the wind was cold enough to give you an ice-cream headache after a short stroll along the rocky, forbidding beach. The cabin had no electricity, indoor plumbing, or interior doors.

Charlie, his wife, Freddie, and their three teenage children slept in the cabin's only room, and when Julia and Paul arrived, they joined them.

Another woman (me) might have objected to the rustic situation in which she found herself. She might have poked her beloved in the ribs and said, "Tell me I did not drive all the way across the country to pee on the freezing beach behind a piece of driftwood?" Even allowing for the fact that Paul and Julia were now drunk on love, sex, and premixed martinis, Julia would have had every reason to do such a thing, having spent idyllic summers at a beach house in Santa Barbara, where the winds were calm and orange blossom–scented, the ocean tranquil and inviting, and the house plumbed.

But Julia was a devotee of anything that was risky, difficult, and had the potential for catastrophe. All the high-wire cooking she would do on *The French Chef* decades later, the boiling of live lobsters, the flipping of omelets, was par for the Julia course. She craved adventure and made it a point to find it wherever she could.

Living in close quarters with the people who meant the most to the man who meant the most to her was Julia's idea of a terrific time. So much could go wrong! So many nerves could become frayed. So much truth about people's genuine nature could be revealed. Still, Julia was fearless; her tactic was to unload both barrels of her entertaining, charismatic Julianess upon the unsuspecting Childs. She made up funny songs with the kids, fashioned hats for them out of strands of seaweed and bits of broken shells, cooked alongside Freddie, chopped wood and cleared brush with Paul and Charlie.

The Childs marveled. It was the summer of 1946, remember. People didn't drive cross-country, much less fly cross-country. It took a lot of effort for a Californian to wind up in a tiny town on Mount Desert Island, Maine. "Out West" really was out there, and the very East Coast, progressive, intellectual Childs hadn't spent much time with Julia's species of westerner—hang loose, raucous, outspoken, with a boundless appetite for novelty. A woman who played each day as if it were a piece of jazz. She whistled while she worked, and she worked as hard as any man. She didn't care that the cold salt air turned her red curls into frizz, or that she was forced to hand-wash her clothes in a pot heated over an open fire. Not only that, and on a completely different topic, they noticed, or at least Charlie did, that she had the longest, most beautiful legs in the world.

As the vacation drew to a close, Paul and Julia announced their engagement. Because Julia was practical as well as unconcerned with propriety, and because it *was* 1946, a time when, celebration-wise, weddings had more in common with Sunday brunch than with a multimillion-dollar Hollywood blockbuster in 3-D, they set the date for As Soon As Possible, September 1.

The day before the wedding, Paul and Julia were in a head-on collision with a runaway truck. They saw the brakeless truck barreling down on them, and Paul tried to swerve, but it was hopeless. They were both thrown from the Buick. Paul hit the steering wheel, Julia the windshield. On her way out the passenger-side door, her shoes were knocked clean off her feet, and her last memory before passing out was that she needed to hang on to those shoes—she loved them, and pretty shoes in her size were so hard to find.

The next day, they were married anyway. A picture from the happy day shows Paul leaning on a cane and Julia looking slim and feminine in a short-sleeved suit with a scalloped, ruffled hem and belted waist. The dinner roll–size wad of gauze taped to her temple does nothing to detract from her serenity and happiness.

⚜

The story of the Childs' courtship is my favorite verse in the epic Song of Julia, the part that occurred a few years before that fateful day in November when the angel Gabriel visited her at the restaurant in Rouen, bearing a plate of light, lemony, delicately sautéed sole meunière, and the message that she would go forth and deliver an entire nation from Jell-O molds jazzed up with pineapple and green beans.

It's the "before" Julia, the California hayseed in her natural state, roaming the world as a single giantess, never passing up an opportunity to engage people, get a little smashed, and have a good time. Julia loved life, even before it started going her way. She had no idea when she married Paul Child that she would score a trifecta: a divinely happy marriage, a career that would both fascinate and challenge her for the rest of her days, and the achievement of fame and glory. She was just being Julia, living with her customary abandon. For those of us who have a complicated relationship to food, a somewhat tortured on-again-off-again love affair with cooking, who don't automatically thrill to the question "What's for dinner?" every morning upon waking, who sometimes wish we could just hook up an IV for a week and not have to deal with it, the Julia without the apron is the simplest, least complicated Julia to love.

My own affection for Julia is more complex than that of the average home cook. For one thing, I'm not the average home cook. I am the below-average home cook. I have a few "signature" dishes (stuff I can make without pulling out a cookbook), but otherwise I am a mere recipe follower, and despite some serious attempts throughout the years, I cannot seem to elevate my game. Every new recipe I try becomes simply another recipe I know, not the gateway to deeper understanding. I'm like a Japanese pop star who can sing an entire show of English songs without speaking the language, or like the algebra student I once was, who can memorize enough equations to pass a class but is still unsure why I'm solving for X. When in doubt, which is about four nights a week, I fall back on roasting a chicken and steaming some broccoli.

Just so we're clear.

How Do We Love Julia? Let Us Count the Ways

Julia is the one true god of modern American cooking. Before Julia (B.J.) it was all cheap, overcooked pork chops suffocating beneath a glop of tepid Campbell's cream of mushroom soup; After Julia (A.J.) it was *Rôti de Porc Grand-Mère* with a zippy little Chardonnay.

God-fashion, she is everywhere. Every time a cook avoids shortcuts, Julia is there. Every time someone is trundling her cart down the wine aisle and thinks, "I'm going to give this Schloss Gobelsburg Gobelsburger Rosé Cistercien a shot!" Julia is there. Every time you toss in another dollop of butter in lieu of the more heart-healthy alternative, you're cooking with abandon, the Julia way. Every time you hop on the scale after having cooked with abandon, and cuss at that ever upward-creeping needle, the name you're really taking in vain is Julia's.

When was the last time you heard or said "bon appétit" and didn't think of Julia Child? Come to think of it, who in America has said "bon appétit" in his or her normal voice since about 1964?*

Oh, I know. History is full of exceptional chefs who were committed to educating Americans about the glory of good eating long before Julia Child came along. Chefs who were more exceptional than Julia,† and who also had their own cookbooks and TV shows. James Beard comes to mind. Actually, he's the only one who comes to mind, as every other good, hardworking, dedicated cook has been thrust into the deep shadow cast by the massive klieg light that was *The French Chef.*

---

* Midway through the second season of *The French Chef.*

† Just because we adore her doesn't mean we've lost touch with reality.

My theory is that our real attachment to Julia is less about her cooking, or even about what she did for the cause of serious cuisine, and more about our admiration for her immutable aptitude for being herself. Julia's real genius wasn't in breaking down the nine million steps in cooking a mind-blowing beef bourguignon, or assembling a thousand-page cookbook,* but in having the confidence to stand in front of a camera, week after week, without trying to change one thing about herself.

Is there anything more radical or attractive? A woman who's not particularly pretty, who's as tall as a man and has a voice like a cartoon character, but who, nevertheless, lives in her own skin with self-assuredness and joy?

During her time at the head of the culinary pack, she certainly had her detractors. In 1966, the year Julia was christened Our Lady of the Ladle on the cover of *Time* magazine† and made the leap from best-selling cookbook author and popular star of a cooking show on educational TV to Most Famous Chef in America, a lesser-known Frenchwoman named Madeleine Kamman, who'd also graduated from Le Cordon Bleu, and who had slaved away in the kitchen in the bowels of a one-star French restaurant and was technically better trained than Julia, sniffed loudly and publicly that Julia was neither French

---

* Not hyperbole. An early draft of *Mastering the Art of French Cooking* was 1,200 pages long.

† In the November 25, 1966, issue the precise wording was "the Lady with the Ladle," a much less poetic coinage that appears in "A Letter from the Publisher." Somewhere along the way the phrase morphed into Our Lady of the Ladle, and it is misquoted as such by *Time* in "The 25 Most Powerful Women of the Past Century" in 2010.

nor a chef. Cantankerous food historian Karen Hess, who made a name for herself by being against celebrity cooks, elite foodies, people who knew nothing about food, and everyone who wasn't her, told David Kamp, author of *The United States of Arugula*, that she thought Julia was a dithering idiot.

I'm sure there were others. Julia may have ushered in the Age of Cuisine in America, but foodie infighting has been around since at least 1765, when a certain Monsieur Boulanger opened the world's first restaurant in Paris and was promptly sued by a local food guild, claiming his single menu offering of sheep's feet in white sauce violated their right to be the only group in town licensed to serve cooked food.*

Every generation imprints on a slightly different Julia. The first knew her as the serious, exacting author of the exhaustive *Mastering the Art of French Cooking*, Volume One, while its younger sisters grew attached to the slightly goofy cheerleader known as "The French Chef," first in black and white, then in color. The Julia of the late 1970s was the one immortalized in Dan Aykroyd's iconic *Saturday Night Live* impersonation; her resultant vaguely Monty Pythonesque reputation had no hope of being rehabilitated by the short, perky spots she did on *Good Morning America* and the often awkward cooking shows that never quite lived up to *The French Chef.* There was a half decade or so near the end of the twentieth century when she fell off the radar. Then, Julie Powell, a girl in a dead-end job

---

* Not much is known about Boulanger, including whether he ever existed.

looking to give her life meaning, single-handedly engineered a Julia comeback by cooking and blogging her way through *Mastering the Art of French Cooking**. Her *Julie and Julia,* which served as the inspiration and template for Nora Ephron's movie of the same name, reintroduced Julia to a whole new, hip home-cooking crowd.

But for most of us, Julia is primarily The French Chef. TV Julia was organized, efficient, yet breezy, with her kooky warble, effortless confidence, and endearingly never-quite-right hairdo,[†] chopping onions, grating cheese, whacking frozen pastry crust with a wooden dowel, giving pointers on the wrist action involved in flipping an omelet, and demonstrating with glee the fascinating, mildly revolting innards of a lobster.

She came off as a woman not unlike her viewers, who, before she became famous, was cozily married to a nice man who went off to his government job every morning while she, in pearls and twin set, puttered around the kitchen. She spent her hours grocery shopping, preparing meals for her husband, hosting dinner parties for his business associates, writing newsy letters to friends

---

* Hereafter to be referred to as simply *Mastering.* I toyed with using MTAFC throughout, but it looks to my eyes like one of those unfriendly military acronyms.

† If there's anything that dates *The French Chef,* it's the obvious and touching lack of an on-set stylist. Julia's coiffure was so flat in the back; given the mania for teased hair in those days, it's hard to believe that one of her assistants didn't think to rush out with a comb and can of Aqua Net and give the back a little volume. But as I write this, it occurs to me that aside from her sister, Dort, who was six foot five, the only people who ever came face-to-face with the back of her head were men. Eventually, Paul struck on the idea of employing a wig—so much easier!

and family, purchasing copper saucepans, and, when she had the time, catching up on her magazines. She was Everywoman, if every woman could thrive in Paris despite speaking almost no French, eat everything she pleased, put in fourteen-hour days for years on end creating a cookbook for which there was, as far as anyone could tell, no market, and, deep into middle age, train herself to cook, instruct, and entertain in front of the camera, something for which in 1963 there was little precedent and no official handbook.

Which is to say that, however average and normal she may have looked, she was like no one else.

Not long after Julia's famous conversion luncheon of sole meunière in Rouen on the afternoon Paul and Julia arrived in France, she enthused to Avis, "I've finally found a real and satisfying profession which will keep me busy well into the year 2000." Julia was a self-professed exaggerator and must have thought, as George Orwell did when writing *1984*, that 2000 was eons away, that people would be vacationing on Mars by then. Instead, she would have exactly that career. In September 2001, at the age of eighty-nine, she would still be in front of the camera, filming a video to run alongside an exhibit of her famous kitchen at the Smithsonian Institution.

Julia was able to convince an entire nation that cooking could be creative and endlessly absorbing because that was how *she* experienced cooking. If there was ever an evening when Julia was feeling tired and grouchy and simply could not bring herself to throw a chop in a pan, it has been lost in the mists of time. For Julia Child cooking was fun, and fun was something Julia, from the time she was a girl breaking into the homes of neighbors just for kicks, never said no to.

I cannot, in good conscience, allow that word "fun" to sit there on the page unmodified. One of the great misunderstandings we hold about Julia Child—the first being that she was housewifey in the aforementioned manner, when really she was Che Guevara armed with a pound of butter and a sauté pan—is that most of us share with her the same definition of fun.

Chances are, if you're one of those people who define fun as any activity that includes a cocktail and putting your feet up, you're not a cook on a par with Julia Child. This is not to say you might not be a devotee. This is not to say that you don't have a few terrific recipes. This is not to say that you refuse to answer the clarion call to pickle your garden's bounty in August or, as we do in my house, spend three weeks baking cookies in December. This is not even to say that you, like me, have been known to be lazy.

But fun for Julia always involved breaking a sweat. It may have involved a few swigs of wine while she worked, but it never involved kicking back. Like people who fancy ultramarathons and Ironman contests hosted in tropical climes, Julia loved endless exertion.

✤

I'm tap-dancing here. Can you sense it? Readers are so sophisticated these days; they can tell when a card is yet to be played, a shoe to drop, when something is being withheld.

Here I am, setting out to write a book about our beloved Julia's many inspirational and aspirational qualities, but, if I'm to be honest, when I say her name—Julia!—I'm not infused with feelings of warmth and joy, but with a low-grade feeling of dread.

My problem with Julia is that it's impossible to extricate her from the main problem I had with my mother, which is that she was an early devotee of Julia. Every time I think about French Chef Julia lustily chopping off a fish head with what she called her "fright knife," or closing her eyes and tasting some beurre blanc, I can smell the buttery, floury, slightly blood-infused smell of browning beef in our yellow and orange kitchen in Whittier, California, not fifteen miles from where Julia grew up in Pasadena. In my memory it is always a day during the triple-digit heat of September, my mother—redheaded, like Julia—red-faced before the stove, stirring and tasting and stirring and tasting and stirring and tasting. Then stopping for a cigarette.

Every morning my mother sat at our Formica breakfast bar, smoked a Viceroy in her orange quilted bathrobe, and planned the evening's menu. Cooking was not easy for my mother, a redhead with fragile skin who suffered from raging allergies to citrus and even carrots, which she was forced to peel wearing rubber gloves.

The longer something took to cook, the more it required simmering, reducing, deglazing,* the more my mother liked it. I think she found the standing and stirring, while puffing on a ciggie, what we would now call meditative. Looking back, I suspect she stood and stirred when it wasn't entirely called for.

I came home from after-school sports practice around five o'clock. At my big public Southern California junior high and high school, it was pretty much an all-comers meet. If you were moderately coordinated and were willing to stay after school every day for practice, there was always a spot for you on the Junior Varsity whatever. I played field hockey, basketball, and volleyball. I was a long jumper on the track team and swam the breaststroke on the swim team. But most of all, when I came home at five, I was starving.

My mother would be standing at the stove, wearing a pair of capri pants and a short-sleeved cotton shirt (not unlike those worn by Julia on *The French Chef*), smoking her Viceroy and stirring. The kitchen smelled of onions and butter, or garlic and butter, or what I know now to have been wine and butter. I'd ask when we were going to eat, and she would say *soon*. But it didn't mean soon. It meant whenever she was finished stirring. My father would come home around six-thirty, kiss my mother on the cheek, and make himself an Old Fashioned. Under cover

---

* Terms I learned only decades later. When I was a surly child watching her cook, I had no idea what was going on.

of his cocktail preparations—the opening of the cabinet to fetch a glass, the opening of the refrigerator to retrieve the lemon peel—I would try to steal a cookie from the treat drawer.* The treat drawer was separated from the stove top by the sink. If I waited until the exact moment my dad opened the fridge, there was a chance my mom would be distracted and I could dip into the drawer and snag a cookie. But usually she saw me coming out of the corner of her eye, reached over, and pushed the drawer shut on my arm. For years I sported matching indentations where the edge of the drawer got me.

We usually ate around eight-thirty. I had finished my homework hours earlier, and some important TV show was inevitably on at that very moment. I had long since stopped being hungry and had entered the state where your body starts digesting its own organs to stay alive. My mom liked to focus on one impossibly difficult Julia dish at a time, so her *Porc Braisé aux Choux Rouges* would be accompanied by Birds Eye frozen squash, the bright orange variety that looked exactly like the baby food I would one day serve my daughter. Her *Tranches de Jambon Morvandelle* was served with frozen succotash.

Even so, it was all the same to me. Unless it was Taco Night,† what we had for dinner was immaterial to me. As it was to my dad, who was the ultimate food-is-fuel guy. But I was not so hungry, nor worried about missing *Sanford and Son*, nor wrapped

---

* In which was stored a loaf of rye bread, a loaf of white, and a package of Van de Kamp's oatmeal cookies.

† Friday nights, unless Mom found a new recipe she was desperate to try.

up in schoolyard drama, that I did not see what my mom was up against: Night after night she went to all this trouble for two people who didn't appreciate her food.

I've come to understand that my mother threw herself into cooking like Julia for complex personal reasons. She'd always wanted to go to Europe, and this was a way of participating, however modestly, in what she thought of as High Culture. I imagine she was also "cooking Julia" because it was creative and challenging, because she knew she was responsible for dinner anyway, and she might as well amuse herself in the process of making it. Hindsight, however, does nothing to change the truth that at the time I was deeply annoyed. I was the one who did the dishes. And what the number of dishes conveyed to me was that what my mother spent the afternoons of her life doing was a hell of a lot of work, for little reward.

As a result, the Julia I prefer to hold in my heart is a strapping California party girl who crowbarred herself out of the comfy life in Pasadena, who forced herself on France and won over the French, the woman who lived with abandon.

LIVING WITH ABANDON, A LA JULIA

Julia's genius for throwing all caution to the wind served her the entire length of her long life. Given that she worked harder than most of us, and believed in rigor and discipline, how did she also live with abandon?

Make the most of the makeshift.

Today, Le Cordon Bleu is an international institute of "gastronomy, hospitality, and management," with branches all over the world. The name itself attracts such words as "elegance," "prestige," "distinction," and every fancy pants modifier that comes to mind. But in 1949, the year Julia enrolled, it had fallen on hard times. Like everything else in Paris, the war had done a number on the venerable institution.

The place was dirty. There was no one around to wash the mountains of dishes dirtied by the students. They were often short of necessary ingredients, including salt. After some haggling with the management, Julia was placed in a class with eleven ex-GIs, most of whom were there in order to learn enough to enable them to cook on the line at a diner back home.

It was as lame and poorly run as it could be, yet it was here that Julia met her mentor, Chef Max Bugnard, here where she discovered her great passion for cooking.

The degree to which Julia learned to cook in makeshift conditions cannot be overstated. There's a famous black-and-white picture of Julia standing in front of her stove in the kitchen at rue de l'Université, stirring something in a saucepan. The stove top hits her at midthigh. So low is the burner, her arm is practically straight. The counters were for "pygmies," as she good-naturedly complained in a letter to Avis DeVoto. Still, here is where she learned to cook.

These days, we've gotten incredibly fussy. With our personal playlists, our complicated made-to-order half-caf, half-decaf lattes, our special mattresses that can adjust for each sleeper, our individually designed college curriculums, we've gotten out of the habit of making do with what's at hand. Part of living with abandon is giving oneself over to one's circumstances without any expectation that things are going to be to our liking anytime soon. We can hope that things will improve, but it shouldn't prevent us from doing what we've set out to do. Julia had an astonishing capacity to be content with what was in front of her, whether it be a cooking school run on spit and a string or a less than perfect hunk of meat. She made do and moved on and rarely regretted it.

Make it up as you go along.
Do you have a file containing a list of lifetime goals for education, career, and family broken into ten-year plans, complete with large-scale goals to achieve within that time frame, and further divided into smaller goals you must reach to contribute to attainment of the larger ones?

If so, you should seriously consider either moving the file into the tiny trash can on your desktop or folding it into an origami flapping bird before recycling it.

Julia, for most of her life, never knew what the hell she was doing. The moment that best exemplifies her inborn laissez-faire attitude occurred at Smith College, where she professed to anyone who was interested (her academic counselor) that her life's goal was to be a "lady novelist" but then neglected to take the only creative writing class offered at Smith.

This isn't to say Julia wasn't highly organized and meticulous with her cooking—perhaps she loved cooking in part because by its very nature it required her immediate attention and focus—but she was always ready to walk through whatever door opened next.

Who could have planned for, or anticipated, *The French Chef*? Even the "bon appétit" was ad-libbed.

Once, during the late 1980s, Julia guest-starred on *Late Night with David Letterman*. Her task was to cook a hamburger. Letterman asked whether she'd ever cooked anything inedible.

"Of course, many times," she replied.

"What do you do then?" he asked. "What happens?"

"I give it to my husband," she said.

Meanwhile, the portable demonstration stove was on the fritz, and the big, bulging patty of ground beef sat cold in the pan. With less than a minute left in the segment, Julia decided to serve it as is, smothered with grated cheese she melted with the aid of a blowtorch she produced from behind the counter. To Julia's delight, Letterman managed to choke down a mouthful of the "beef tartare."

Bon appétit!

Make this your mantra: I'm never too anything for anything.
Maybe it was because Julia's mother, Caro, thought her daughter could do no wrong. Maybe it was because Julia was always the tallest person in the room (beginning with her Montessori preschool class), or because she was old (thirty-seven) when she discovered her passion for cooking, or because she was very old (fifty-one) and very tall and had that cartoon voice when she hit it big as The French Chef. But if she wanted to do something, she did it.

When she landed on the shores of France in 1946, she spoke only high school French, and bad high school French at that. Her teacher had pronounced her accent "insurmountable."

Still, she plowed ahead.

Julia was so at home in her own skin, it never occurred to her that whatever was going on with her or whatever people thought of her would be a reason to refrain. If she had the energy and the interest—and when did she not?—she was up for it. ATV riding at seventy-two. Impromptu trips abroad at eighty. She was an early adopter of technology, especially the laptop, which allowed her to work while on airplanes as she was rounding the bend to ninety. In 2000, four years before she died, she was trading wise-cracks with her friend, chef and cookbook author Jacques Pépin on their cooking show, *Julia & Jacques Cooking at Home.* "Are you going to toast our buns, Jacques?" she famously wondered on the hamburger episode.

Julia arrived at "just do it" as a personal credo long before Nike snapped it up. Nothing anyone thought about her could stop her. Imagine a life in which you're never too anything for anything. Never too old to go back and get that degree. Never too uncoordinated to cut loose on the dance floor. Never too wrong-of-body to wear that swimsuit and throw yourself into the waves.

RULE ^{No.} 2:

PLAY THE EMPEROR

✣

*I'm all for hunger among the well-to-do.
For comfortable people, hunger is
a very nice quality.*

IN 1992 JULIA WENT TO LONDON TO ATTEND THE OXFORD
Symposium on Food. She traveled with Nancy Verde Barr, who
served as the executive chef for Julia's *Good Morning America*
segments and helped her produce her feature articles for *Parade*
magazine. Anyone who worked with Julia for any length of time
inevitably became a good friend, and Barr had been with her for
a dozen years by then.

Julia almost never said no to an invitation. Even in her dot-
age, the only thing that prevented her from saying yes to every
invitation that came down the pike was the scant twenty-four
hours in every day. Just as the two friends were preparing to leave
for England, the London branch of Cordon Bleu invited them
to another event, and Julia, a traveling pro with everything she

needed packed into a small black suitcase, insisted they add it to their itinerary. But where would they stay? As luck would have it, Julia's friends—the Sullivans—were traveling in the States at the time, and their very nice flat remained empty.

What could be more perfect? Especially since this would allow Julia and Nancy to throw a cocktail party for their London friends in the cooking world, of which Julia had many.* One night, at the end of their stay, Julia thought it would be nice to thank their generous hosts by photographing themselves enjoying the flat, and enclose the pictures in the thank-you note. Then she spied a rare porcelain vase sitting on the mantel—but one of the Sullivans' large, priceless collection—and hatched a better, much more entertaining plan.

Inside their proper thank-you note the Sullivans also received a handful of photos of Julia and Nancy . . . in their bathrobes pretending to hurl their museum-quality porcelain to the floor. Ha!

Julia was eighty when she carried out this caper, and it was far from her last.

There are many stories like this about Julia, by those who knew her well and those who knew her in passing. What they all attest to is one of the great mysteries surrounding the person

---

* From here on out, please just assume that unless otherwise specified the person in question is one of Julia's friends. For her entire life, wherever Julia went, she had many friends. Friends who would come over and cook with her, friends who would throw her parties, friends who would travel with her, friends with whom (and on whom) she could play practical jokes. So many friends, that a normal person would be exhausted by all this human contact, but not Julia.

of Julia Child: She grew up without losing those tremendous kid-type qualities that make everyday life fun.

NOTHING PREVENTED JULIA FROM BEING HERSELF

Until the day she died, Julia was never out of touch with what my friend Gabby calls her "girl spirit." For most women that curious, rambunctious, prank-playing, singing-at-the-top-of-our-lungs-while-riding-our-bikes-down-the-middle-of-the-street *joie de vivre* begins to dwindle around the time we start reading *Seventeen,* and is usually extinct by the time we're in the throes of calorie-counting, expensive eye cream–wearing, eligible man–pursuing adulthood. We can hardly be blamed. I can't think of an era in which Julia's exuberant tomboy style of behavior was ever in vogue for grown women. Being yourself in the way Julia was herself has been frowned upon as being unladylike, un-Joni Mitchell-like, or un-smokin' hot babe-like, depending upon the era. This wouldn't matter in and of itself, except the implication of being a woman who inhabits and expresses the full range of her personality, as inevitably put forth by the pundits-du-jour, is that refusing to get in line with accepted notions of femininity means you're bound to wind up unloved and alone.

Once, when I was in my mid-twenties, the age at which it becomes clear that you really *are* an adult, and not the faux-adult to which people give lip service the day you turn eighteen, I had a rare, candid conversation with my dad.

The operative word here is *candid.* My dad and I talked quite a bit for a father and daughter of that time. In many ways, we were comrades-in-arms, united in our mystification at my mother's compulsion to make complicated French food and her kooky extroversion.* He taught me how to drive a nail, win at checkers, draw a correctly proportioned human head, ride a horse up and down a steep hill, and shift gears in my Volkswagen without engaging the transmission. Our many conversations were topical: the Civil War, rattlesnakes, gold mines, football vs. basketball, movies, the origin of words, and the nature of infinity. My point is he wasn't one of those coldhearted, disinterested dads (like Julia's, as it turned out) who had no relationship with his child. We talked a lot, just not about anything personal.

But one night while I was sitting with him, "enjoying" an after-dinner drink—he was fond of the horrid licorice-flavored, urine sample–colored Galliano—I felt compelled to unburden myself of a complaint I had vis-à-vis the way he and my mother had parented me. Since we were both adults now, I figured it was time he was enlightened.

I said that my mother, now conveniently dead and not there to defend herself, had ruined my confidence by telling me, around age twelve, that I could no longer do all the stuff I really liked to do, like, for example, laugh so hard I was forced to throw myself on the floor, rolling around holding my belly;

---

* The woman was known to make friends in the produce department at the A&P and was a devotee of the Halloween party long before adults went in for such things. Like Julia, she loved a party more than anything and would have thrown many more than she did, except that my father loathed a party more than anything.

or do headstands in the living room while we had guests; or get into fistfights with the boys with whom I disagreed; or beat everyone in the entire school at tetherball. Her fear was that if I didn't rein it all in a bit I would deprive myself of a successful and happy teenhood, which translated to never having a boyfriend, which further meant I'd be scarred for life.* I told my dad that there was nothing worse than allowing me complete freedom to express my personality and then once I hit eighth grade suddenly insisting that everything everyone thought was so cool about me—my impersonation of a goat, for example†— was inappropriate behavior for a young lady. I confessed that I had been tortured by this for years. I said it was an inner conflict so pernicious it was threatening to send me to a psychiatrist.

"At twelve, suddenly, I was supposed to become someone else!" I'd raised my voice. I'd sounded strident. Another big no-no.

"You're right," said my dad. "We should have sat on you much earlier."

Sat on me?

Only many years later, after I had become the parent of a child who took umbrage with some of my own parenting, did it occur to me that my dad was probably joking.

But regardless, Julia never had to deal with anything remotely like this. No one ever tried to sit on her, even in jest.

---

* She wasn't necessarily wrong; I know many adults who can in less than a minute access the deep anguish they felt at not being asked to the prom.

† It was so authentic I could confuse a herding dog.

She marched straight into womanhood with the best parts of her character intact. There was no Reviving Ophelia phase, where her self-regard plunged as she reached adolescence, no transition from high school to college, then from college out into the real world, that was rocky enough to transform her from the brightest, brattiest, most ebullient girl in town, into a shy woodland creature who worried that everything she felt, thought, and did was somehow not right.

The result: She was a woman never divided against herself.

I'm sure there are men who feel divided. But I'd wager it's usually because of choices they've made, not because up until puberty they were perfectly acceptable human beings, at which point they had to completely rewire themselves to become attractive to the opposite sex. Do you know one forty-year-old guy who, deep in his heart, feels he's too old for *Star Wars*? And does a love of *Star Wars* prevent him from getting laid (maybe, but not if he's discreet) or walking down the aisle? On the other hand, a woman of the same age who holds the same attachment for the things of her childhood might just have a mental disorder.

Look at pictures of Julia. Never will you see on her face an expression that conveys anything approaching self-doubt. Never in her eyes will you catch that vague look of self-consciousness so many of us possess, even beneath our extra-whitened HD smiles, that telegraphs our basic discomfort with the person we're projecting. By all reports, the feeling expressed on Julia's face at any given moment mirrored the feeling in her heart.

Pretty much everyone who knew Julia said the same thing: that what you saw was what you got. She had no buried girl self on which her proper woman self had been constructed, and, perhaps not incidentally, she had no regrets, except one: When she was a nonagenarian, long after Paul had died, and her health was forcing her to slow down to three times the speed of a normal healthy fifty-year-old, she did remark to her old colleague and cowriter Simone Beck that at this stage of her life it would have been nice to have a grandchild or two around. Otherwise, until the end of her life, she was as gregarious, energetic, pragmatic, curious, and adventuresome as she'd been as a child.

How did she turn out this way? And more important, is there any way we can reverse engineer our own lives in order to see whether we might extract any Juliaesque essence that will help us live as fully and gaily as she did?

Be rich.

My inclination is to lay Julia's stupendous self-acceptance and *joie de vivre* at the feet of her equally stupendous privilege. Julia always maintained that her family was of the Buick not the Cadillac class, but she grew up with an upstairs maid, a gardener, and a cook. They also had a tennis court, which suggests the McWilliamses were neither of the Buick class nor the Cadillac class, but the class of people who are so well off they don't know that having a private tennis court means you're really well off.

Julia's dazzling mother, Julia Carolyn "Caro" Weston, was from Massachusetts and an heiress to the Weston Paper Company. Her father, John "Big John" McWilliams Jr., was a Princeton man who moved to Pasadena from Illinois, to take over his father's land management business. Managing land in Southern California in the early part of the twentieth century could apparently make one quite wealthy.* Pasadena was a small town in 1912, the year Julia was born. By Southern California standards, it's loaded with history. The first football game that became the Rose Bowl matchup was played in 1902. Around the same time, enormous resort hotels sprang up along the board boulevards—the Raymond, the Huntington, and Hotel Green—and a raft of gargantuan churches of all denominations sat on their corners, surrounded by queen palms.

John and Caro, with their three children, Julia, John III, and Dorothy (known as Dort), lived in several grand houses, including a huge five-bedroom, five-bath colonial, designed by architect Reginald Johnson, famous locally for also designing the Los Angeles Opera House, Santa Barbara's Biltmore hotel, and several Episcopal churches. When the McWilliamses weren't relaxing at home, you could find them at one of three country clubs they belonged to: one for swimming and riding (Valley Hunt Club), one for golf (Annandale Country Club), and one for polo (Midwick Country Club).

---

* What do land managers do? No idea. Whatever it is, it pays better than, say, managing an apartment building or an Office Depot.

Pop, as Julia called her dad, was a brusque Presbyterian Republican. He was civic-minded, believed in public service, and did many good things like run the Pasadena branch of the Red Cross and sit on the chamber of commerce, but he was so conservative that anyone who didn't grow up the way he did, think the same way he did, and hold all of the same values he did was a traitor to the nation.

Julia adored Pop in the standard manner of worshipful daughters everywhere, but lucky for her she was temperamentally like her mother, having inherited "the Weston twinkle" from Caro, whose disposition was as sunny as her husband's was stern. A sassy redhead, at Smith College (class of 1901) Caro was the captain of the basketball team and had a reputation as an independent thinker. She didn't marry until the advanced age of thirty-three, believing it was important to see the world before settling down. Even after she became the mother of three, she spent a good part of every day playing tennis. Endorphins weren't discovered until 1974, but clearly Caro McWilliams enjoyed the benefits.

Caro loved to cook in the manner of people who aren't required to do it every day. Dinner generally consisted of some kind of overcooked meat and boiled potatoes. Because Caro always instructed Cook to include a vegetable grown in their garden, and perhaps some sliced avocado from one of their trees, her reputation among Julia's friends was as a health food nut. By the time Julia was in her teens, Cook would also have been able to purchase Heinz Ketchup, Van Camp's Pork and Beans, Del Monte canned fruits and vegetables, Grape-Nuts,

Wheaties, Welch's Grape Jelly, and Wonder Bread. Because Julia never went into the kitchen if she could help it, and as an adult had almost no memory of the food she ate as a child, we don't know whether she ever tore off the crusts of a slice of Wonder Bread and rolled the white part into a ball.

Caro had a few noteworthy recipes: baking powder biscuits, Welsh rarebit, and a Yankee specialty, codfish balls, made from poached dried cod whipped with egg and mashed potatoes. She would cook these at least once a month, usually on Thursday, Cook's night off. When Caro was too tired from her daily tennis, or simply not in the mood, the McWilliamses would repair to one of their "dining clubs." But Caro's "love" of cooking notwithstanding, she never pressured her daughters to learn to cook, unlike my own mother who, a week before any school vacation, would promise she was going to teach me to cook a few things when I was on break. Nothing sounded more punishing. Do you know who cooked? Boring mothers, that's who. The first day of vacation I would leap on my bike right after breakfast and disappear until it started getting dark, and I knew she would start calling around to my friends' houses to tell their mothers to send me home for dinner. Once she worried that no one would want to marry me if I didn't know how to cook, to which I sneered, "*Good.*"

Whether Julia and Dort McWilliams could or couldn't cook was immaterial; as adults they would have enough money to attract a suitable mate, or live high on the hog as eccentric spinsters. In any case, they would have their own Cooks.

When I was an undergrad at the University of Southern California, there was a special, appalling football cheer trotted out in the fourth quarter, when it looked as if the Trojans were going to lose. "Whether we win! Whether we lose! We're rich, we're rich, we'll buy you!" I doubt Julia's parents harbored such crass notions, but the sense of entitlement was there in the heartbeat of the house, in the complete freedom that Caro accorded her children, especially her daughters, girls who were average-looking and born to be taller than almost everyone else in the room. Because they were wealthy in love, attachment, and money, they didn't need to be pretty, petite, and docile, predictable bait for a future husband that would improve the family's fortunes.

Disclaimer

Once I sat on a panel at a book festival, where the topic was how to fashion a productive writing life. My copanelists were celebrated first novelists who, it was said, came from money and were married to money and did not suffer in the way that so many writers do, holding soul-sucking day jobs, or cobbling together freelance gigs that pay on a regular basis (and without fail pay ten or more months after the job is complete). They were lovely, intelligent women with shiny hair, well-turned ankles, and solid habits, and just enough specific requirements (a special type of bendy straw for their Diet Coke, an ergonomic chair) to show how seriously they took their creative temperaments. I, who prefer to cultivate the foreign war correspondent mode of creation, training myself to write anywhere at any time with anything at hand, was in equal parts impressed by their awareness of what "worked" for them and appalled by their fussiness.

A woman at the back of the room raised her hand. She was the mother of very young children. Even from that distance you could see her exhaustion in the slump of her shoulders. It didn't help matters that she was wearing an earflap hat and fingerless gloves. As it turned out, my lovely copanelists were also the mothers of very young children, and the question asker wondered if they had any advice about how she, the mother of toddler-age twins, might also fashion a productive writing life.

One of them suggested hiring a nanny for the morning hours, and the other said, "You must get yourself an office out of the house. With the recession, I'm telling you the rents are *cheap.*"

Disbelief registered on the woman's face. An invisible thought bubble floated above the heads of pretty much everyone in the place: It may be cheap for *you.*

After having written about the McWilliamses money and the McWilliamses' five-bedroom yellow colonial and the zany, loving mom and reserved but mega-bread-winning dad,* and the love and freedom Julia experienced every day of her life, I wonder if I sound like the lovely debut novelist—well-meaning

---

* Best not to mention the summer homes in Santa Barbara and St. Malo, an exclusive development near Oceanside, where, to this day, the homes, modeled after a French fishing village, are passed on from one generation of Sepulvedas, Doheneys, and Chandlers to the next.

and completely out of touch. Obviously most of you have not enjoyed anything close to Julia's fabulous upbringing. Yes, there's some misery to come, but by and large it was as good as it gets. Until they invent the way-back machine, we're all stuck with who and where we came from.

Still, Julia's life wasn't perfect.

Live in a temperate climate.
Money makes our childhoods so much easier, except when it screws us up; were it not so, the phrase "poor little rich girl" would never have entered the vernacular, nor would the hearts of the nation go out to Suri Cruise, with her tiny designer heels and peculiar father.

But no one can argue with the salubrious effects of nice weather, in this case in Pasadena, California, pre–internal combustion engine. Here, then as now, there are no brutal seasons to interrupt the fun, no frigid winters paralyzed by blizzards, nor humid, daze-producing summers. Those old adages that worriers from other, harsher climes live by have no meaning in Southern California. "Make hay while the sun shines" and "Save your money for a rainy day" is advice for someone else, someone whose world is not their oyster.

If you have a good childhood, it's a very good one in that climate, where the weather cooperates to the extent that the world seems benign and supportive of all human endeavor, where you can play outside all yearlong and no one ever yells "Don't forget your mittens." In Pasadena, twelve months a year, excluding three rainy weeks in February during an exceptionally wet season, you spend your entire life outdoors, bombing around on your bike. The world, with its golden light and dry air, does nothing to impede your desire to play. The message is that nothing in the natural world, aside from perhaps an earthquake—which is short, to the point, and cannot be predicted—will ever get in your way.

The fine weather colluded with Caro to support Julia's junior-anarchist style. She was a freewheeling tomboy who loved to hike, swim, play tennis, and golf. Julia was the girl in the neighborhood who could pitch a softball overhand.

"Jukes" was full of ideas for adventures that were rarely evaluated for their merit. The point of her young life seemed to be to make something, anything happen, regardless of the outcome. I should stop here and say there's a flip side to living in such an agreeable climate. Living in a world unmarred by the threat of impending weather, cloudy on occasion but with no chance of snow, ice, or sleet, does make a kid feel that if anything exciting is going to happen, she's going to have to be the one to make it so.

Above all, Julia loved not knowing what was going to happen next. From the time she was a girl, her eyes popped open in the morning and one of her first thoughts was *How can I have fun and make some trouble today?*

She was the ringleader of the neighborhood group of kids who, completely unsupervised, rode around the oak and pepper tree–lined streets, up into the scrubby hills, down into the dusty arroyos, and over the newly built bridges, where they would stop only to drop mud pies on cars passing below.*

They routinely stole material from construction sites and broke into vacant houses in the neighborhood. Mrs. Greble, the neighborhood "witch" (she yelled at Julia for hiding out in her oak tree, smoking Pop's purloined cigars), was the target of Julia's pranks. Once they broke in and stole a chandelier and buried the crystal prisms.

Sometimes Julia would get caught, and then she would get dutifully spanked by Pop, but did it make her feel bad for what she'd done? Did it make her refrain from stealing Pop's cigarettes, cutting the braids off the head of the pastor's daughter, or hanging out with the hobos down at the train yard? Not at all. For Jukes getting spanked was simply the price of doing what amused her.

By the time she was a preteen, Julia had developed a habit of stealing Pop's cigarettes, and also the cigarettes that belonged to the parents of her friends. Pop, who by this time had recognized the futility of traditional discipline, instead gathered his kids for a powwow. He promised that if they stayed away from cigarettes until they were twenty-one, they would each receive a thousand-dollar bond.† Julia, recognizing a great deal, abstained until the stroke of 12:01 a.m. the day after her twenty-first birthday, then

---

* On second thought, maybe Jukes's mom did try to force her to learn how to cook, and that's how she found herself doing all this cool stuff.

† One thousand dollars in 1925 is worth $13,218.11 in 2012 dollars.

smoked a pack a day well into middle age. She gave it up briefly on July 26, 1954, and took it up again on July 27, 1954, failing to see any reason then why she should deny herself the pleasure.

Play the emperor.
When she wasn't breaking and entering, or seeing what happens when you melt a piece of pavement tar on the stove, Jukes wrote and performed her own plays. She was entranced by the local community theater and would go with her mother by streetcar into Los Angeles to catch the latest Charlie Chaplin "photoplay," as movies were then called. From grammar school on up she acted in any play that would cast her, and it was here she learned an intractable lesson, one that couldn't be mitigated by freedom, affluence, or the love of Caro and Pop.

Julia was simply too tall to play the female roles.

Too tall to play the damsel-in-distress, too tall to play the lady-in-waiting, too tall to play the ingénue or the princess. If she wanted to participate—and when did Julia ever not want to participate?—she would be forced to accept the roles usually reserved for boys. Thus, she was cast as a lion or other large, fierce beast, or as the emperor. At Katharine Branson, the college preparatory school she attended before going to Caro's alma mater, Smith, she played Michael the Sword Eater in a production of *The Piper*.

Even as a girl Julia was tremendously adaptable, and once she realized she would never play a princess, she found she preferred playing the emperor, with his great strides across the stage, his roaring proclamations. As the emperor, she was free to indulge her inner ham, something she would never be able to do otherwise. She was free to be herself.

Julia's height informed her life, in the way being a McWilliams of sunny Pasadena ultimately didn't. At age four she was the tallest girl in her Montessori school. She would be, for the rest of her life, among the tallest, if not the tallest, person in any crowd. In her beloved France, she would be a foot or more taller than everyone she met.

A woman as tall as Julia could never be transformed by a new dress or tube of lipstick. No makeover would ever make over the part of her that failed to comply with traditional standards of feminine beauty.

To what degree did it bother her? To what degree did she try to slouch or smoke in order to stunt her growth—actually, she may have smoked in part for that reason—or wished upon a falling star that one day she would wake up to find herself a foot shorter? Probably not at all. Julia was never one to indulge in "what if." She never pined for the impossible; if there was one thing that nothing could be done about, it was her height, and fairly early on she made peace with it.

Her practical nature asserted itself, and she realized she had a choice. "Why languish as a giantess when it is so much fun to be a myth?" she wrote in her diary. She may have been whistling in the dark, or practicing a sassy attitude, but she seemed to have understood, even then, that a girl could choose to behave in a way that would distinguish her. Perhaps that was her only choice, given the alternative was to "languish." Still, given how sociable she was, how free-spirited and energetic, she knew this was something she could pull off. By sheer force of her personality, she could escape her fate.

Years later, she could joke about it. When she and Paul moved into their apartment at 81 rue de l'Université, their bed was so short, Paul built an extension, about which Julia said, "At last, I could fit my size-twelve feet comfortably under the covers, rather than have them sticking out like a pair of gargoyles."

Once in a great while, she was distressed by the way she looked. As she was rounding the bend to forty she would write to Avis DeVoto that whenever she read *Vogue* she "felt like a frump . . . but I suppose that is the purpose of all of it, to shame people out of their frumpery so they will go out and buy 48 pairs of red shoes, have a facial, pat themselves with deodorizers, buy a freezer, and put up the new crispy window curtains with a draped valance."

Julia was able to deconstruct the disingenuous motives that drive women's magazines with the ease she normally reserved for deboning a duck, seeing quite clearly that while ostensibly offering inspiration and useful advice, the stories and articles quietly pummel the reader's sense of self, the better to drive her into the arms of the advertisers.

What is most instructional about this little anecdote, however, is that even by average woman standards, Julia's sense of style was pretty basic, mostly because how could it be otherwise, given that it was next to impossible to find any skirts, trousers, blouses, or jackets in her size. Even with the help of a series of good tailors, the pickings in the shops and department stores were slim. Only when she read *Vogue* did she feel a little frumpy, even though, in actuality, she was a lot frumpy. But her ability to accept, work with, and even celebrate her own idiosyncrasies made the truth of the matter irrelevant.

Change nothing.

One of the trends that caught fire in the wake of the most recent global recession is the Buy Nothing movement. It goes by a variety of names—The Compact, the Minimalists*—and there are various cells and offshoots, but the point is to reduce debt and clutter, to recycle, reuse, and simplify, and also to help defuse our panic over having no disposable income, or perhaps any income at all.

There are the inevitable blogs about living a year without buying anything, and websites where people post about their experiments in growing and canning their own tomatoes and using the recycled newspaper from Starbucks as toilet paper, and also, confess when they "slip." A whole argument can be made about how the health of the global economy relies on consumers breaking down and buying a pair of shoes once in a while rather

---

* Two young cute guys named Joshua Fields Millburn and Ryan Nicodemus who've made careers for themselves being two cute guys with a basic website and no stuff.

than foraging for them in the Dumpsters behind the dorms the day after the students have gone home for the summer, but that's another polemic for another time.

Inspired by the Buy Nothing people, let's resolve to Change Nothing about ourselves. By now, most first-world women don't even need to go online, pick up a magazine, look at a billboard, or turn on the TV; we've completely internalized the message that everything about us can be improved, and that if we're not actively working on the endless remodeling project that is Us, then we lack self-esteem. That every last one of us can and should be thinner, firmer, smoother, more radiant, more supple, more plump in the parts that are supposed to be plump and less plump in the parts that aren't, with lots of swingy shiny hair up there and no hair down there, barely warrants mention, so old-school is that brainwashing.

In recent years the wheel has turned a little. Women's magazines have heard the criticism that every woman on the planet who reads them for any length of time winds up despising herself so thoroughly that her options have been narrowed to throwing either the magazine or herself off a bridge, and so now their focus is "spiritual."

Now, while effortlessly rocking our skinny jeans, we must also be working to live a life of abundance, and to recognize said abundance, and to learn how to feel properly grateful, and to become the hero of our own journey. Wait, your inner critic is somehow as resilient as a post-apocalyptic cockroach and keeps chiding you for failing to be the hero in your own journey? Not to worry; here are eighty-seven foolproof ways to silence that inner critic.

On and on it goes. Julia wasn't having any of it, and neither should you.

Here's an experiment: For one day, walk the earth in your fat pants and raggedy cuticles. Do whatever you do in the morning to get yourself together, beauty-wise,* then, forget about it. If you're not feeling grateful, then don't be grateful. Quit practicing whatever inner thing you're practicing. Don't take the stairs instead of the elevator. Don't choose the banana instead of the bag of chips. Every time that chiding little voice inside says you should be working on changing yourself, silence it. Instead, play the emperor. The emperor doesn't live on an endless self-improvement regime, and the emperor doesn't apologize for who she is. And as for the inner critic, our *bête noire du jour*. If there's nothing to criticize, she's out of a job. Do this, for one day, and see what happens. Sometimes, simply accepting our imperfections serves to lay the groundwork for confidence. Who knew?

I'm not saying you're fine the way you are. Julia, certainly, for her time, was not "fine" the way she was. Instead, by embracing all that she was, she redefined fine.

---

* This isn't a back-to-the-earth retro-hippie screed; I love my Chanel mascara.

RULE <u>No.</u> 3:

LEARN TO BE AMUSED

⚜

One's best evenings are composed of a good dinner, and nothing else is necessary.

IT WAS NEVER OBVIOUS TO ANYONE THAT JULIA McWILLIAMS would make anything of herself. Neither the most observant teacher nor an empathic, crystal ball–reading college career counselor predicted any kind of real career for Julia, much less a groundbreaking, world-changing one.

When Julia entered Smith College, Caro's alma mater, in 1930 at the age of eighteen, she was that wild roommate you love to death but can't live with because you fear flunking out.* Then as now, there are no dormitories at Smith; rather, every student is assigned to a house with other students from all four grades. Gilley, the housemother at Hubbard House, where Julia lived, kept notes on her charges, and about Julia she wrote, "A

---

* Her more studious roommate, Mary Case, was forced to move out.

grand person generally but she does go berserk every once in a while, and is *down* on all 'Suggestions and Regulations.'"

Northampton, Massachusetts, with its refined culture that valued the arts and intellectual pursuits, was a world away from provincial Pasadena, and Julia felt acutely like the huge galumphing Westerner that she was. Once again she was the tallest in her class (of 634); once again she was faced with the stark choice of whether to be a wallflower or a myth. It was a difficult adjustment, but Caro came east over Thanksgiving and took Julia shopping in New York for the requisite preppy wardrobe—crew neck sweaters, tweed skirts, saddle shoes, and pearls—and once she looked the part of a proper Smithie, she was able to devote herself fully to what she loved most, causing trouble.

For Julia, her first two years of college were an extension of high school, with the exception of an added bonus: The local speakeasy was within walking distance of Hubbard House. She spent her time partying and continued to specialize in pranks large and small. Moment to moment, if there was an opportunity to do something unexpected, to change the course of the next five minutes, Julia did it. Her impulse to engage, to get involved, to mix things up, to see what happens when you do x instead of y was compulsive. If there was a chance to lock someone in or out of a room, she would do it. Anything that involved having to climb out a window was right up her alley. When her roommate, Mary, hung a rug between their beds so that she could study, Julia would toss jelly doughnuts over the makeshift wall. I'm sure modern psychiatry has a name for this compulsive need to disrupt, distract, and get a laugh. It made Julie, as her classmates called her, popular. Her professors observed her sparkle and spunk; they appreciated her vivacity, but felt she lacked the ability to persevere. She was not serious.

Caro had been a basketball star at Smith, but Julia lacked both the drive and the aptitude.* Although she did play tennis, hockey, and baseball and ride horses at some nearby stables. She was a solid C student her sophomore year and enjoyed a somewhat outlaw reputation among her friends for failing to care. They had no idea that for Julia's father, good grades equaled being an intellectual equaled being a communist, and if there was one thing worse than a communist . . . well, in Pop's world, there was nothing worse than a communist. A serial killer who voted Republican was better than a Democrat with the Nobel Peace Prize.

None of this really mattered until junior year, when the young women were expected to declare a major, which mostly served notice to those who weren't dating anyone steadily to buckle down and focus on their husband hunting. Despite the heady academic environment at Smith, most of the students were there to find a proper husband, culled from their male counterparts at Amherst, Yale, Harvard, Princeton, and Columbia. Girls who landed a guy were rarely motivated to graduate.

---

* One of the great misconceptions of basketball is that being tall is enough. Julia was an enthusiastic athlete, but not a particularly coordinated one.

Getting engaged and dropping out within the same week wasn't uncommon. And on the slim-to-nonexistent chance a newly minted Mrs. *did* want a job outside the home, the only real career that promised advancement, a decent salary, and prestige was teaching, which was subject to the so-called marriage ban, a federal law that prohibited the hiring of wives.

Why women who were expected to spend their lives overseeing the help needed to be conversant in Homer and Descartes was never discussed. Even Sophia Smith, who founded the college in 1875 with money inherited from her father—". . . with the design to furnish for my own sex means and facilities for education equal to those which are afforded now in our colleges to young men"—never quite addressed what the young women who would benefit from her largesse were actually supposed to *do* with the education they received there.

First, Julia declared a history major, then decided that maybe she would be a "lady novelist" instead. She was in a more precarious position than most; as popular as she was with her classmates and even her professors who, if not impressed with her scholarship, still admired her "savoir faire," the young men of the Ivy League just weren't interested.

One of Smith's vocational counselors suggested that since marriage was obviously not in the cards for Julia, and since her family was well-off, she would not need to pursue a career, or even have a job, but could devote herself to charity work. Even the brain trust at Smith believed Julia's sole option was to return home to Pasadena and join the tribe of Ladies Who Lunch.

A Brief Reflection on the Merits of College

Before moving on to Julia's inopportune early adulthood, let us pause to appreciate how her college education, an excellent one by all standards, did next to nothing to inform her future. Throughout her life Julia adored her alma mater and was a devoted alumna until the day she died, but while she was an undergraduate there, she may as well have been at the University of Southern California, my alma mater and the local party school of choice for many Pasadeneans. There was no reason for Julia to be at Smith, other than that her mother went to Smith. Like so many four-year colleges, Smith was merely a four-year holding tank for Julia, while she matured not at all.

And that was okay.

My intent is not to put anyone out of a job who has made a lucrative career consulting with high school seniors and their energetic parents about how to find the perfect college; how to prepare to take the SATs and ACTs;* how to compose a brilliant, provocative essay;† how to create a standout application;‡ and how to present a top-notch case for admission using every tool in your family's personal arsenal of awesomeness, but if the life of Julia Child tells us anything, it's that where you go to college doesn't matter.

---

* Multiple times, usually.

† But not too provocative.

‡ Complete with incisive line-by-line critique.

I'm not trying to console you because your kid didn't get into HYPS* or her first choice, or your beloved alma mater. Nor am I saying it to make you feel better because, gentle reader, you'd dreamed all your life of going to NYU and you wound up at a state college, and now you worry that you'll never achieve anything. Steven Spielberg attended no famous film school but the California State University Long Beach. Conversely, a friend's brother-in-law graduated from Harvard and now is a checker at Trader Joe's.†

What matters is what's going on with the student, and if you're young, naive, and "unserious," as Julia would describe herself years later, and without any real interests, where you wind up is irrelevant. "I only wish to god I were gifted in one line instead of having mediocre splashings in several directions," wrote Julia in a letter home to Caro near the end of her college career.

"Passing tests doesn't begin to compare with searching and inquiring and pursuing topics that engage us and excite us," said the esteemed philosopher and cognitive scientist Noam Chomsky. Julia passed the tests, but all the searching, inquiring, and pursuing was decades down the road.

In June, after commencement, she drove Eulalie home to California, accompanied by her mother, sister, and brother, who'd taken the train across the country to meet her. It was the summer John Dillinger was on the loose. Eulalie's top speed was forty

---

* Yes, there's an obnoxious acronym for the so-called top schools: Harvard, Yale, Princeton, Stanford.

† Not unhappily, I might add. Still.

miles an hour. At home, in balmy Pasadena, Julia played tennis and golf and threw huge parties where she secretly spiked the punch. She enjoyed herself. Still, she was too much the daughter of practical, tough-minded, hardworking John McWilliams. In 1935 she went back East, where she enrolled in the Packard Commercial School to learn "secretarial skills"; after a month the tedium drove her bonkers and she quit. She eventually found herself in New York City, working in the advertising department of W & J Sloane, a home furnishings store. She was good at her job, organized and able to get along with just about anyone. In her small apartment she subsisted on Birds Eye Frozen Food.*

Despite her success at W & J Sloane, Julia struggled in New York. She felt "big and unsophisticated." She fell in love for the first time with a "literature major" named Tom, who was in New York looking for work. She was smitten; he was only kind of smitten. She was a bull in the china shop of love, falling over herself to assure him of her love and devotion, probably he was her first lover. Eventually, he wound up betraying her by up and marrying a fellow classmate from Smith.

Even the boisterous, seemingly indestructible Julia McWilliams was knocked sideways by love. She wanted to go home. When she gave her notice at work, telling her boss she was moving back to California where she belonged, he sputtered, "But Julia, I can make you the biggest advertising woman in New York!" To which she replied, "I already am."

---

* Invented in 1923 by Clarence Birdseye, with a $7 electric fan, a bucket of brine, and a cake of ice.

In Pasadena, all was not well. Caro had suffered from chronic high blood pressure for years. In the 1930s, high blood pressure was thought to be a natural part of aging; the heart needed to beat harder to squeeze the blood down those aging, narrowing arteries, so it went untreated. But after Julia returned home, the normally spirited Caro started complaining of headaches. One day Pop rushed her to the hospital with a raging fever. The doctors brought down her fever and declared her well, but something wasn't right. She suffered from dizzy spells and nausea, and her skin had taken on a yellow pallor. Caro's entire family, both parents and five siblings, had all succumbed to the ravages of high blood pressure, and on July 21, 1937, only a few weeks before Julia turned twenty-five, Caro did, too. Julia was beside her when she died.

Julia was lost. It was as if at the age of twenty-five she retired. Her youth, which had yielded nothing much in the way of discovery about who she was and what she should be doing, seemed to be behind her. In the fall, after Caro was laid to rest, Dort returned to college at Bennington and John returned to college at Princeton and Julia was left, as the oldest daughter, to "take care" of Pop. As the McWilliamses live-in domestic staff had grown to include a housekeeper, cook, butler, and several gardeners, there was nothing for Julia to do, really, but keep her increasingly difficult father company. I'm being gentle; the man was grief-stricken. The truth is, by all reports, Pop was a nasty-tempered bigot, who grew only more so after Caro and her humanizing influence departed. Conservative doesn't begin to describe his hatred for anything that resembled change. He despised anyone from the East Coast, Europe and Europeans, Democrats and moderate Republicans, intellectuals, and the brand-new Pasadena Freeway that connected his personal utopia to the corrupt metropolis of Los Angeles. Julia loved her father, and she had grown up tolerating his tirades, but her time living and working alone in New York had changed her in ways that she could not yet quite understand. All she knew was that there was a big world out there.

Pop gave Julia an allowance, and from her mother's estate she inherited at least $100,000* and a nice wad of IBM stock. Julia was rich, unencumbered, and could do whatever she wanted. This sounds like a recipe for happiness, and yet Julia was not happy.

Every morning the sun rose from behind the San Gabriel Mountains, eased across the southern sky, and then set over the Pacific. Every morning Julia played a few rounds of golf at the exclusive Annandale Country Club with Pop, joined friends for lunch, and played another round of golf or perhaps some tennis. Then she showered, dressed, and repaired to the even more exclusive Midwick Club—whose ultra-right, ultra-rich members included Walt Disney and Will Rogers—where, in the afternoon, she would drink martinis with people she claimed to find entertaining. "All I want is to play golf, piano and simmer, and see people, and summer and live right here," she wrote in her diary. Later, she would remember these long months as being the only time in her life she felt completely lost and confused.

---

* That's a lot; about $1.6 million in 2012 dollars.

She spent the next five years this way. Now there was no question that Julia was being left behind. Her friends from Smith who, before, were merely married, now were having children. Mary Case, her college roommate, had a daughter and named her Julia.

I feel so enervated by the reality of this part of Julia Child's life that I'm having a hard time finishing this section. She roused herself after a few years of golf, martinis, and nightly dinners in which she submitted to Pop's rants against Democrats and every other child of Satan* and snagged a job writing a fashion column for a short-lived magazine called *Coast.* Then, she briefly held a job at the West Coast branch of W & J Sloane, from which she was fired. She joined the Junior League, the *Junior League,* where she starred in various children's plays (playing, always, the lion, the big scary beast, or the emperor).

How did the woman who became Julia Child suffer through years of such soul-crushing inertia?

You Don't Need to Have the Life You Want to Enjoy the Life You Have

It's a little hard to feel sorry for Julia, given that by twenty-five she was pretty much set for life. What I find exciting about this

---

* Even then Julia loved to talk about politics, but Pop forbade disagreement; if she ventured to open up a discussion, he left the table.

is that if Julia's life was any indication, being set for life turns out to be excruciatingly dull. Evidently, a boatload of money is no substitute for love and a sense of purpose. I would say this is obvious, except that millions of people spend their lives trying to figure out how to get more money, when perhaps time would be better spent trying to figure out what it is that only you were born to do, like revolutionize the concept and practice of cooking in America.

But we're getting ahead of ourselves. It would be decades before Janis Joplin immortalized the lyrics "freedom's just another word for nothing left to lose," but that was pretty much the position that Julia found herself in, turning the bend toward thirty. The one man she'd ever loved had jilted her, her beloved mother was dead, her siblings were far away, she was stuck alone with her impossibly sour father, and she had no genuine interest in anything. All her money did nothing to change this. Julia loved life most when it was busy, frenzied, and unpredictable, and yet without quite knowing how it happened, she'd become one of the Ladies Who Lunch.

Still, as restless and disheartened as she was, she didn't make an effort to change anything. She "simmered," waiting for something, she knew not what. She was desperate for a change but somehow knew better than to make a change simply for the sake of it.

In August 1940, at the age of twenty-eight, Julia received a marriage proposal from Harrison Chandler, the scion of the *Los Angeles Times.* Chandler was handsome, ultra-conservative, and boring. He and Julia traveled in the same country club martini-drinking circles. From the outside he appeared to be the perfect match, and Pop, who rarely took an interest in his daughter's life except to berate her for her left-leaning politics, was eager for her to say yes. Here was a chance for her to escape her fear of becoming an old maid, confirm her desirability as a woman, please her father, and solidify her upper-crust social standing by becoming part of one of the first families of Southern California.

She said no.

She knew she was lost, knew she was spinning her wheels, knew she couldn't possibly imagine what the future might hold. She didn't know if or when things were going to get better. Perhaps to convince herself that her life was going well she wrote in her diary, "I am quite content to be the way I am—and feel quite superior to many a wedded mouse. By God—I can do what I want!" And still, she didn't do anything to change her circumstances.

With our modern dust mote–size attention spans and belief that the mark of being human is not our pair of opposable thumbs but the ability to be happy all the time, the moment we're discontented for longer than forty-eight hours, we start casting around to see how we might remedy the situation. We know from our favorite self-help gurus that the only thing that's permanent in life is change, so why not help life along and engineer those changes ourselves?

Maybe we need a new job, a new apartment, a new boy-friend, a new diet, a new haircut, a new gym, a new book group, or Botox. The next time this occurs to you, rather than resolving to get your act together or your ducks in a row or do something that you imagine your future self will thank you for, do nothing.

Instead, learn to be amused, and find things that give you pleasure. It feels like an old-fashioned concept—to spend time doing things that have no self-improving component, that are done simply for the pleasure of doing them.

Men have an easier time amusing themselves than women do. I'm resisting the urge to qualify this. I don't know one woman who is as good at messing around as are all the men I know. Men joyously go out to find a pickup game of basketball. They maintain a monthly poker night without losing a wink of sleep. Men watch the game, happily waste endless hours playing Halo and Grand Theft Auto, read comic books, and build model trains. The biggest male workaholic I know still religiously maintains a quarterly weekend wine tasting/hiking date with an old friend. Do you do anything remotely like this? I don't.

Women, when they aren't taking care of their families or working, spend their "free" time improving themselves. They go to the gym, shop, get their nails done, or rededicate themselves to eating clean or meditating often. That most of these endeavors are aimed at improving how we look I'm going to let slide for now. My point is that finding ways to amuse ourselves can make our otherwise unsatisfactory lives, satisfactory. If only for now.

What are some amusing things to do? Golf, tennis, horse-back riding, Dance Dance Revolution, and anything else where the only reason for doing it is pure enjoyment. Jigsaw puzzles. Karaoke. Nothing too crafty, because that veers into the home improvement arena. Cooking a huge, complicated meal out of *Mastering* is also a terrific idea.

I have a few dishes, recipes that are good and that I can repro-duce more or less every time I make them. They are:

- Chicken enchiladas

- A sausage risotto recipe from the *New York Times Magazine*

- *Côtes de Porc à la Liégeoise* ("cheesy pork chops") from *The New York Times 60-Minute Gourmet,* by Pierre Franey

- "My" Spaghetti, adapted from *Eating Together: Recipes and Recollections,* by Lillian Hellman and Peter Feibleman

- Some broccoli salad thing with grilled red peppers from *The Greens Cookbook,* first made during that week I was a vegetarian

- Roast chicken

Like every pretend chef, I'm basically an "assembler." The French gastronome Brillat-Savarin once punished his cook for serving him a limp, sad piece of sole, enraged that she dared to produce a meal without the faintest understanding of the science behind cooking. That clueless cook, *c'est moi.*

It's Easter and I've decided to make Julia's beef bourguignon, the only recipe I make that my mother also made, the same classic dish Julie Powell, as played by Amy Adams, ruined so spectacularly in *Julie and Julia* by falling asleep on the sofa and leaving it too long in the oven.

Beef bourguignon isn't really a spring dish, except in northern places like Portland, where it's still cold and wet well into April. Our corner Whole Foods* doesn't have small onions; they only stock them for the big winter holidays. When you think of all the types of inedible greens they display so effusively year-round, it doesn't seem like a lot to expect they would have something as basic as a small onion. I settle for frozen, feeling a flick of irritation because this is what my mother used, back when red onions were considered exotic.

Beef bourguignon was the only Julia dish my mother made that I found acceptable, but I only cook it maybe once a year because doing so makes me so sad that when I'm done I can rarely bring myself to eat it.

During my first semester of college my mother, who was only forty-six, was diagnosed with brain cancer, an astrocytoma with the shape and reach of a starfish. All that summer and fall, before her diagnosis in December, she suffered from crushing headaches and double vision. Her doctors decided it was an

---

* Hereafter referred to as Whole Paycheck; self-explanatory.

underactive thyroid, then hypoglycemia, then the garden variety symptoms of menopause. Her headaches persisted, and now, thinking back, miraculously, so did her elaborate nightly meals. There is no summer longer than the one before college, where your old life has wilted but your new life is yet to bloom. In the afternoons, I watched my mother wash down three aspirin with a swig of Coors before getting something on to simmer. How on earth did she manage this, and why? It's still a mystery to me. I'm one of those home cooks who comes down with the sniffles and consequently orders takeout for the next week.

They were able to remove part of her tumor, but only part. The prognosis was dire. My mother, according to her surgeon, woke up, looked him straight in the eye, and "asked all the hard questions." She was given six months to live, but only managed three.

By February she had completed her prescribed rounds of radiation and chemotherapy. My parents had been steadfast in shielding me from the horror of it all. I was a mere seventeen. I'd gone away to USC, my father's alma mater, pledged a sorority, and was dutifully having the time of my life. They insisted.

My birthday is March 2, and suddenly, uncharacteristically, my father called and summoned me home. Both he and my mother wanted me to come home on the Sunday before my birthday for dinner.

Of course I would be happy to come home for my birthday. Home meant presents, cake, and my choice of fancy dinner. In the naive way of children to whom nothing bad has ever happened, I assumed that if my mom was cooking me birthday dinner, then she was better and was going to be okay. She couldn't talk very well after her brain surgery, so my dad had taken my birthday dinner request.

The fanciest special-occasion food I knew was steak and baked potatoes with sour cream and chives, and that's what I asked for. Also, a green salad with Bob's Big Boy Bleu Cheese dressing. I knew there would also be some kind of store-bought cake from the grocery store.

But that Sunday, the moment I walked in the door, I took one whiff and knew we weren't having steak. It was that smell I knew so well: the buttery, floury, slightly blood-infused smell of browning beef on a too-warm day. In Southern California a March birthday is sometimes an early summer birthday, and the dining room windows were open, and sun filtered through the dark pink bougainvillea that grew thick on the trellis over the patio. My mother was setting our places at the big dining room table, one utensil at a time. She wore her usual capris and a bright floral top, and an orange turban to hide what she called her "bald chicken head." She shuffled in with a fork, set it on the table, shuffled back into the kitchen, rooted around in the silverware drawer, then shuffled back into the dining room with a knife.

I felt the sense of injustice rising up in me. It wasn't fair! They'd called and asked what I wanted and I'd said steak and there was no steak. Instead, my mother was cooking beef bourguignon. I didn't even dislike beef bourguignon, but it was not steak. All these years later I can still summon the deep rage I felt that day, like any expert method actor you care to name. No steak. No baked potato with sour cream and chives. No green salad with Bob's Big Boy Bleu Cheese dressing. And also, no cake. And soon, no mother; the person I loved most in the world was leaving me.

I followed her into the kitchen. We didn't talk. We never talked anymore. She leaned against the counter, her redhead's pale complexion mottled and her face slack and puffy from her meds, removing each piece of beef from the pan with the focus and precision of someone defusing a bomb.

I think she made a few simple things before she died a week later, but Julia's beef bourguignon was the last thing she made for me.

When I made the dish last Easter, I rushed through the browning of the stew meat, ruining my favorite hoodie with splattered oil. I also wound up with an extra plate of sautéed carrots and onions. I spent my late teens and most of my young adulthood furious that my mother solicited my opinion about what I wanted for my birthday dinner, and then didn't cook it. Then I moved into a phase where I realized I was really angry not at her menu planning but at her for dying and leaving me alone, for that is how I thought of being left with my well-meaning silent father. Now that I have lived past the age at which she died and have a daughter older than I was when she got sick, I can only imagine the sheer terror she must have felt at the thought of dying, and of leaving me to make my way in the world without her.

Then, in a further iteration, over the course of the long Easter afternoon while I stood in front of the stove turning and basting the beef at a slow simmer, I found myself admiring her courage. Her days were numbered and she knew it, and she was going to spend her last days at the stove making something that gave her pleasure.

What is it about beef bourguignon? Really, it's just beef stew braised in red wine, an ancient peasant dish from Burgundy that married up. Auguste Escoffier, the father of modern French haute cuisine, described the basic recipe followed by most of us; Julia modified it; Judith Jones, Julia's editor at Knopf, mastered it, as did my mother, as did Julie Powell, as did I. How many of us are simply home cooks, how many lost daughters? How many, like me, shove food in the oven and then run out the door and down the block, in an effort to get as far away from the kitchen as possible?

Rule No. 4:

Obey Your Whims

⚜

. . . you've got to have a what-the-hell attitude.

Julia may have been sheltered and unsophisticated, but she was also observant and empathic, and when she worked at W & J Sloane in New York and was paid $18 a week, she realized how tough it would be for the average working person to make ends meet.* She wasn't very political, but she saw that there was a lot more to the world than the country club lifestyle in Pasadena.

But for the bombing of Pearl Harbor on December 7, 1941, Julia might have remained in Pasadena for the rest of her life, golfing, drinking afternoon martinis, throwing parties, playing the role of the pampered spinster daughter of one of the richest, most unfriendly men in town. Part of Julia would have enjoyed

---

* Her parents sent her a weekly $100 allowance, which she put in her savings account.

this. She adored Pop, rationalized his obstreperous personality as part of the "he-man" temperament, and from the time she was a child she was not against the pursuit of pleasure. But another part of her longed for hard work and a devotion to something bigger than herself.

When America entered World War II, Julia woke up. When President Roosevelt, whom Pop despised, put out the call for women to join the war effort, Julia followed her first impulse, which was to do . . . something. One of her abiding qualities was a belief in spontaneity, and the power of acting on a whim.

First, she signed up to volunteer for the local Aircraft Warning Service, but that didn't quite do it. She worked for the Red Cross and then went on—what the hell—to take the civil service exam. She was determined to do something meaningful, and she applied to join both the WACS (Women Army Corps) and WAVES (Women Accepted for Volunteer Emergency Service). On her applications she shaved three inches off her height, claiming to be six feet tall, but she was still rejected due to "physical disqualification."

That hurt. It was one thing to be overlooked for the princess roles, which included fiancée, dewy bride, young wife, and busy mother, and another to be rejected by the military, which, you would think, would welcome someone as fit and strong and, yes, tall, as Julia.

Undaunted, and unwilling to relinquish her first impulse, Julia left Pasadena for Washington, where she was eventually hired as a junior research assistant for the OSS, the precursor of the CIA. The OSS was itself something of a whim, an ad hoc organization tossed together in June 1942 by the Joint Chiefs of Staff, who admired Britain's Secret Intelligence Service, MI6, and felt that upon entering the war, the United States needed its own espionage agency.

Led by General William "Wild Bill" Donovan, attorney, soldier, and football star at Columbia, the agency was staffed mostly by Ivy Leaguers and educated eccentrics with an adventurous streak. Donovan liked to hire people of independent means, under the adorable assumption that the rich were less likely to be bribed than someone who needed the money.

Julia worked in the Registry, where she functioned as an elevated file clerk, keeping track of classified information. Even this is less glamorous than it sounds; basically, she worked from morning 'til night typing index cards.

One day some gossip reached her that the agency was preparing to open an office in India, and Julia, who had never been out of the country except for a day trip to Tijuana, was desperate to go somewhere, anywhere, and India seemed like as good a place as any. Julia was a perfect fit for the OSS. Not only was she a Smithie of means, she was also someone who, as we know, was down on Suggestions and Regulations. They saw her as someone who would be willing to do whatever was necessary.

In March 1944, Julia crossed the Pacific aboard the USS *Mariposa*, with three thousand men and eight other "crows," as the women were called. Their mere presence caused pandemonium, which Julia partially suppressed by spreading the rumor that they were all missionaries. It took thirty-one days to travel from California to Calcutta, during which Julia played enough bridge to last a lifetime and volunteered as a reporter for the shipboard newspaper. She also had her eyes opened.

Julia knew she was undereducated more or less by choice, but was still throttled by the sheer brain power and sophistication of the "eggheads" she met, first on the ship and then at her eventual postings in Kandy and Kunming, China. Social scientists, psychologists, biologists, historians, and journalists; anthropologist Gregory Bateson, then married to Margaret Mead, became her shipboard drinking buddy. Julia didn't know it yet, but she'd found her tribe.

The moment the *Mariposa* docked in Calcutta, Julia received word that she was going to be transferred to Ceylon, where a new outpost was being established in Kandy, under the leadership of British Admiral Lord Louis Mountbatten. Julia would be in charge of setting up the Registry there. She lived in dark, dank quarters that flooded a foot and half every time it rained hard (every afternoon), with a small refrigerator in the living room, on top of which sat a two-burner hot plate.

The longer she did her job, the less she liked it, but she was a trouper. She was her father's daughter; she believed in leaning into the task at hand. She believed in toughing it out.

She claimed that her long hours left her no time to "scintillate." This wasn't quite the case. There was actually plenty of "scintillating" going on; in the small community there were forty males for every female. It was paradise for every single woman but

Julia, who was popular in the way she had always been: a good sport who knew how to have fun, but never a romantic prospect.

Despite her cushy upbringing, Julia possessed a hardy constitution. Before joining the OSS she spent her stamina on the usual upper-middle's pursuit of entertainment and pleasure. Once she was assigned to head the Registry in Kandy, she discovered that she also possessed a remarkable ability to tolerate monotony and discomfort, often working ten hours a day, six days a week.

Her job was at once critical and murderously dull, tasked as she was with handling, cataloging, indexing, and filing every piece of intelligence that passed through the outpost. The OSS didn't just gather information, it also carried out myriad clandestine operations that included spreading misinformation, infiltrating local political organizations, acts of counter-espionage, and pretty much everything we've come to expect from spies vis-à-vis Hollywood movies; to do all this, the operatives needed sometimes speedy access to material, which is where Julia and her secure-yet-easily-navigated filing system came into play. Throughout her life, Julia downplayed her role in the war, claiming to be a mere file clerk, but her high security clearance tells another story.

You Never Know What You Might Find at the End of an Impulse

One of the great satisfactions of casting our gaze back on the whole of someone's life is being able to see where the twists and turns led, and how events given scant attention during their unfolding paved the way for bigger things, sometimes even the biggest things in their lives.

The largest fork in Julia McWilliams' road was her meeting Paul Child, which never would have happened had she not followed that first whim to answer FDR's call to arms, and the second whim that led to her putting in her application to be sent to India. All along the way, and without a thought, she followed her heart. But meeting Paul, who not only changed her life but also gave her a brand-new one, was only part of the yield.

By casting her lot in with the OSS, Julia gained confidence, grew up, met the kind of people with whom she would spend the rest of her life, and also, somewhat bizarrely, learned to cope with vast amounts of important bits of information, an underappreciated and homely activity that over time exercised the muscle that, years later, would allow her to build complex recipes. It turned her into a woman who could write a massive, comprehensive, many-thousand-page cookbook that would revolutionize an entire nation's attitudes about food, cooking, and eating.

When to Heed a Whim

The current flavor of positive thinking, which holds that if we just assume something we desperately want is on its way as long as we "put it out there," has never captured my imagination. Maybe it's because I spent too many Decembers as a child fervently hoping, as a common Christmas Eve myth holds, that my dog would talk to me at midnight. Every year I'd wait for Smitty, our surly black dachshund, to open his mouth and hold forth, and every year he sat curled in his bed giving me the side eye. One year, I even curled up beside him on his little plaid bed and started conversing, hoping that maybe he just needed some reassurance; what I got was a snarl instead.

But embracing the power of the whim is a way to shake things up that nudges life into tossing something unexpected in your path. It's employing your psychic divining rod, allowing it to lead you in a direction where something good, or at least different, is bound to enrich your life.

When I started thinking about whims in general, my first thought, unimaginatively, was the impulse buy. The random candy bar tossed in the grocery basket at the checkout counter; the cute little bracelet thrown atop the sweater at the department store register.

One friend said yes one night when she received a phone call from the Obama campaign asking whether she'd be willing to spend the five weeks leading up to the election working in rural Pennsylvania. On a whim, she said, she left her husband and kids and went.

The best time to heed a whim is when we find ourselves stuck in life, when putting one foot in front of the other is only taking us further away from where we want to go, even though we don't know where that is. The most accomplished whim-follower I know is the twenty-year-old son of a friend. Last year, unhappy at college, where he was taking classes that meant nothing to him, he told his parents he was not returning for his sophomore year but was instead moving to Barcelona to live with some family friends. Barcelona was great for a month, until he met some people who sang the praises of Prague, where he went and worked in a coffee shop for a year. There, he also met a girl, whom, after a time, he followed to Seattle, where he is now working in yet another coffee shop and preparing to return to college. This young guy is of the whim-following age, although from what I can tell, most young adults, with the awful pressure on them to decide on a career path by sixth grade, are too frantic with worry to succumb.

The thing about whims is that most of the romantic ones involve a serious outlay of cash. Even hopping in the car for a weeklong road trip across a state or two will set you back a few hundred dollars; here on the West Coast one of the whims that makes you feel like your life is not in a rut—"let's go to Mexico!"—will set you back thousands. You used to be able to dream about the sun on your face on a Monday, and by Friday your toes were wriggling in the sand at Puerto Vallarta. Now, you'd have to be a part of the 1 percent to afford those tickets.

THE ONE RELIABLE WHIM

The most obvious whim, given the subject of this book, is what to eat. Every day we're faced with satisfying a food or cooking whim. Because when it comes to cooking I'm tortured with ambivalence,* my culinary whims are perpetually at war with each other. On a daily basis, I experience opposite urges. I long to both flee the kitchen† and devote myself to cooking in Julia-holic fashion. But my behavior is purely whim-driven.

Nothing was left to chance in my mother's kitchen. She wrote out her weekly menus on Sunday and shopped for the week the next day. Monday night was pork chops; Tuesday night was hamburger pie, a stewed tomato–heavy take on Shepherd's Pie, with hamburger substituted for lamb, and including frozen French cut string beans; Wednesday night was reserved for "something new"; Thursday was beef stroganoff or beef bourguignon or something that involved simmering; Friday night was Taco Night; Saturday night was Chef's Salad; Sunday night was pot roast. I live in a permanent state of rebellion against this regimen. The thought of writing out a weekly menu makes me want to tear off my clothes and run down the middle of the street, so slavish and restrictive does it seem. My cooking life is all whim, all the time. Even before my kids went off to college, I would often find myself standing in the middle of

---

* I do blame my mother's death, perhaps unfairly, for all of my cooking neuroses. I harbor an irrational belief that had she lived, I would have been able to rebel like a normal teenager, then I'd have come round to the fact that she was a fantastic cook and she would teach me her secrets, and we would stand together beside the stove with identical wooden spoons, stirring identical simmering Julia-inspired sauces, laughing and planning what we would sauté and simmer next. Maybe after getting a mani-pedi.

† Possibly until they invent an affordable meal-in-a-pill, which I would take over a jet pack any day.

the kitchen at 5:30 p.m. wondering what to make for dinner, waiting for my taste buds to speak up. Sometimes I would race to the corner Whole Paycheck for a rotisserie chicken and broccoli. Sometimes I would throw open the cupboard and make Something with Noodles. Sometimes I would make "breakfast dinner." Sometimes, in a burst of inspiration, I would make something fabulous, coq au vin or grilled halibut. Sometimes, we would just go out. I prefer to think this refusal to plan means I've embraced the French attitude about eating. I'm allowing the spirit to move me. Unfortunately, the spirit is not as epicurean as I would like it to be.

I envy people for whom cooking is their true, abiding creative outlet, people who arise every morning and as their coffee is brewing plan what they're going to cook that day. Julia famously said, "People who like to eat are the best people," and presumably she's not talking about the people who stand in the middle of the kitchen eating Wheat Thins with a squirt of aerosol cheese.

When Nora Ephron died, Joan Juliet Buck, who played Madame Elisabeth Brassart, the director of the Cordon Bleu, in Ephron's *Julie & Julia,* wrote a droll, fond remembrance of her friend for *The Daily Beast,* in which after extolling her Renaissance woman genius, she said, "She also had a real life, two early marriages and then one great one, and two sons, one of whom I know and adore. And she cooked."

And she cooked.

There are few three-word sentences that so perfectly evoke a superior sort of down-to-earth femininity. Nora Ephron cooked. This did not mean she threw some Annie's white cheddar mac 'n cheese into a pot of boiling water and emptied a bag of pre-washed romaine hearts into a bowl and called it dinner, like some people I know. Nora cooked, which meant she was warm, generous, sexy, sensual, passionate, and life-loving.

There's a little shop not far from my house that describes itself as "a home decor and flower store in Portland, Oregon, offering a clever mix of modern, vintage, and organically inspired products." Among the clever inventory are cookbooks where every author is a windswept blonde who looks as if she stepped straight from the pages of Robert Redford's Sundance catalog, in jeans or a vintage dress, her white chef's apron tied snugly around her waist. And she always has a waist, this hip and competent cooking beauty, giving testament to her ability to spend her life cooking fantastic food, but never eating too much of it.

If I could genetically modify myself, I would make myself over as one of those people who feels joy at the thought of food every minute of every day, in the hopes that I might capture some of the joy that everyone who loves to cook—and everyone who enjoys cooking *loves* to cook—seems to have. Am I the only one who's noticed this? These days there seems to be an unspoken competition among people who consider themselves to be cooks. No one says "Sure, cooking's okay," or "Yeah, I like to cook," or "Cooking's a nice way to pass the time," or

"Sometimes I'm in the mood to cook, but just as often I could go for take-out Chinese." These days, cooking is a sacred calling that must be pursued with religious zeal. So intense is even the home cook's love of cooking that Jerrod, the man of the house, and I have devised a TV cooking show drinking game wherein every time a contestant proclaims his or her passion for cooking we drink. Fifteen minutes into every episode of last season's *Master Chef,* we were slurring our words.

I read and admired Bill Buford's *Heat: An Amateur's Adventures as Kitchen Slave, Line Cook, Pasta-Maker, and Apprentice to a Dante-Quoting Butcher in Tuscany* about his own obsession with cooking (unlike me, he suffers no tortured ambivalence), and the time he spent working in the kitchen of super-celebrity chef Mario Batali. Once, after a long and brutal shift,* he rhapsodized: "I was a member of a team of cooks, closed away in this back room, people's knives knocking against cutting boards in the same rhythmic rocking way: mine as well; no windows, no natural light; no connection to the outside world; no idea, even, what the weather might be; only one phone, the number unlisted; unreachable—a great comfort, surrounded by these intense association of festive meals."

I long to be one of these passionate people, but I can't help but wonder whether they possess the same passion for kitchen cleanup, because that crap ton of work accompanies every great meal ever made unless it's this one, perfected when I was a junior

---

* The only kind there is in the kitchens of super-celebrity chefs.

in college and had my first apartment and had vowed never to learn how to cook:

Saucisson Hebraïque Nationale en Fourchette Plongé dans la Moutarde Dijonnaise

Ingredients
1 all-beef hot dog (best you can afford)
Grey Poupon mustard

Skewer hot dog on fork, cook over gas burner, unscrew top of mustard, dip hot dog in mustard, stand in the middle of the kitchen and eat.

Several summers ago we hosted an exchange student from Spain. Her gift to us upon her arrival was a small cookbook featuring authentic tapas recipes. Little did Lucia know that one of our favorite local haunts was a tapas place; that her host family was, in fact, a little mad for tapas.* We decided we were going to have a Spanish-American tapas-themed Fourth of July. There was going to be *Patatas con Chorizo* (potatoes with chorizo) and *Tortilla con Alcachofa y Jamon* (artichoke and ham tortilla), *Pinchos Morunos* (pork brochettes), and *Tartaletas con Pisto Manchego* (ratatouille tartlets). We also made four batches of Lucia's

---

* Tapas come from the Spanish word *tapar,* meaning to cover. They were originally slices of cheese or ham used to cover wine cups to keep out the flies.

favorite, *Croquetas de Queso* (cheese croquettes), as well as a few other things I've forgotten. Creating this feast required every cooking implement we have in the house, in part because Jerrod, who fashions himself a great cook when he's in the mood, is also impaired when it comes to eyeballing how big a bowl or pan one might need for any given mixture; if a dish like, say, the *croquetas*, requires something to be mixed, then browned, there will always be at least two extra too-small bowls and pans per cooking step.*

The tapas feast was memorable because it was delicious, and also because it took me four hours to clean the kitchen, including using a butter knife to scrape the flour/water paste† off the counters, stove top, table top, refrigerator handle, and yes, ceiling. The kitchen was over a hundred degrees and I was sweating like . . . a person cleaning the kitchen in the middle of summer, when turning on the oven makes as much sense as turning on the furnace.

And yet, we hear nothing about this from all these passionate cooks, home and professional alike. Do they all have a personal dishwasher? Who scrapes and scrubs and loads and unloads the machine and swabs down the counters and the floors and scrapes the flour/water paste off every blessed surface with a butter knife? Because that takes me at least as long as it does to cook something.

---

* Julia advised: "Always start out with a bigger bowl than you think you'll need."

† If you or your children have ever made a papier-mâché piñata or giant monster head for the school play, you'll know the stuff I mean.

Never mind the three minutes it takes to eat it.

Even Julia once said, "I do love to cook. I suppose it would lose some of its glamour if I were married to a ditch digger and had seven children, however so." Meaning, of course, if you had to cook for that many people day in day out, there would be so many dishes to do you would lose the will to live, much less cook.

Julia tossed off seven as the number of children it would take to dampen the glamour of cooking, but in my experience it takes only three, plus one father-in-law. Yes, I have done my time as a galley slave. For a half decade I was married to a guy with kids, and our blended family was comprised of my four-year old, his five- and eleven-year-old, and his father, who lived with us for a year while doing some contract work for the phone company in Portland. In their defense, my husband and my father-in-law ate whatever I put in front of them. Indeed, they ate *a lot* of whatever I put in front of them. A dozen enchiladas would be hoovered up before I'd returned to the table with the napkins. Seconds, and thirds, were the rule of the day with spaghetti, mac 'n cheese, anything that could be self-served with an overflowing ladle. Another woman might have felt gratified; instead, since I was also the alpha breadwinner at the time, I marveled at how fast thirty bucks worth of organic free-range chicken breasts could disappear.

Every night I tried to make something that everyone could tolerate, since we'd laid down the law that what was for dinner was what was for dinner. The kids could choose not to eat it, but that was all there was to eat. I would spend hours creating menus that took into account one kid's hatred of red meat and fruit, another's hatred of fish and pasta (except plain, with salt and butter), and another's hatred of chicken and all vegetables. I felt like I was training for the World Rubik's Cube Championships, and no one was ever satisfied.

The kids learned to circumvent our strict law against saying "Yuck" when faced with what was for dinner by developing their inner food critics. Not a minute after they'd each taken a bite or two, one would say, "I don't really care for this steamed broccoli, it's a little rubbery." Or, "Pork chops aren't really my cup of tea, but if they were, I'd say these were a little tough." Or, "If I was a veggie burger person, which I'm not, I'd say this one could use a little seasoning."

I've come a little far afield here. My point is this: If your relationship to food and cooking is largely positive and uncomplicated; if, unlike me, you harbor no tortured ambivalence in relation to cooking, then every day provides at least several wonderful opportunities to follow a whim. It's a little thing, opting to make beef pho when you thought you were headed in the direction of a nice lasagna, but it keeps your impulse-following muscle in good shape for the day when something more momentous comes your way.

THE WHIM LIKE NO OTHER
Given the stupendous success of the marriage they created, it's hard to imagine the degree to which Julia and Paul were

ill-suited for each other. Look up the word *sophisticate* and there
you might find a picture of Paul Child. He was also an accomplished photographer—some of his pictures are in the permanent collection at the Museum of Modern Art—and his various
positions during the war always involved "visual presentation,"
mapmaking, or designing and creating war rooms. In the 1920s
he'd hung out with artists in Paris, painted movie sets in Hollywood, taught sailing, and in pretty much all ways lived the
kind of peripatetic life immortalized by Hemingway, minus the
bullfighting and big-game hunting. He was a black belt in judo
and read books in their original French. He wore a cravat.

By the time he was assigned to Kandy, he was forty-four
years old and still reeling from the death of the great love of
his life, Edith Kennedy, a small, chic intellectual twenty years
his senior, with whom he'd spent the last seventeen years. Even
though they'd been desperately in love, they were bohemians
and had no use for traditional marriage.

Still, Paul thought about love more than the average sixteen-
year-old girl. Every night while he was stationed, first in Kandy,
and later in Chungking and Kunming, he wrote to his brother
Charlie, parsing the various charms of the women on the base.
He was persnickety about the traits he required in a mate, but
once he thought he'd found someone who met his standards, he
had a habit of pouncing. He fell in love with Rosie Frame, the
child of Chinese missionaries, who was fluent in Mandarin and
recruited by the OSS to infiltrate Chinese social circles; and with
San Francisco socialite and wild-child Jane Foster, who would in

1957 be indicted for being a Soviet spy; and outdoorsy Marjorie Severyns, who hailed from Yakima, Washington, and loved hiking and double entendres. They were all very young and had their pick of the various young, dashing scholars, reporters, and intelligence officers. When Marjorie threw Paul over for a married man, and not just any married man, but the same one who stole the heart of an earlier crush, Paul became depressed.

Paul liked Julia, even though she wasn't his type. He found her to be warm, droll, and fun to pal around with, but neither well-read nor worldly enough. Once they had a conversation about Gandhi, and Julia said she thought he was a horrible little man and didn't know what all the fuss was about. If this boneheadedness wasn't enough to put him off, she also possessed a somewhat frantic virginal quality that communicated to him that regardless of her good qualities, she was simply too much of a fixer-upper.

Julia, provincial as she may have been, wasn't stupid. In a letter she would write years later to Avis DeVoto, she characterized their main difference thus:

"He is an intellectual, as I interpret the word . . . meaning he is interested in ideas, and is ready to dig for information and is always trying to train his mind (like with General Semantics), and has a thirst for knowledge. Me, I am not an intellectual, though I had 4 years of college. But the people I admire most are the intellectuals; I am trying to train my mind, which is sometimes a fuzzy sieve."

Near the end of the war, in early 1945, they were transferred first to Chungking, then to the medieval city of Kunming, at the rough, mountainous end of the Burma Road. Kandy was a five-star resort compared to Kunming, where the electricity was less dependable, the city outside the station more dangerous, the mud beneath their feet during the rainy season more fetid. In their quarters, they had no furniture aside from army cots. The war felt closer here; on the other side of one of the mountain ranges that surrounded the city on three sides, warlords led peasant armies in skirmishes against the Japanese. Outside the walls of the field station, the citizenry took advantage of the general chaos; there was smuggling, kidnapping, extortion, and a thriving black market.

Except for suffering from unrequited love for Paul, Julia thrived; difficult circumstances brought out the best in her. Without breaking a sweat, she organized and managed the new Registry and was in charge of doling out the opium with which to bribe Chinese officials. The caramel-colored block arrived in a diplomatic pouch and was stored inside the Registry safe.

Paul's love interests came and went, but Julia was always around and available to drink vodka or venture out for a hike around the rice paddies or a visit to a local temple. Together they ventured forth and discovered authentic Chinese food. It was beyond adventurous. Chinese farmers fertilized exclusively with night soil,* and every meal was inevitably accompanied by a chaser of dysentery. Paul had been averse to playing Pygmalion, and yet he found himself visiting Julia's quarters most evenings, sharing books, poetry, music, and art with her.

The war ended first in Europe, then in the Pacific, and in 1946 Julia McWilliams was awarded the Emblem of Meritorious Civilian Service for her "cataloging and channeling a great volume of highly classified communications," a nice honor that had absolutely no bearing on her status as the old-maid daughter of curmudgeonly John McWilliams. After she was discharged, she returned to his house in Pasadena, more or less back where she started from.

She may have appeared to be the same Julia—big, boisterous, golf-playing, martini-swilling, content to sit at the dinner table while her father ran through his usual political rants—but Paul Child was in her head and in her heart.

She'd observed his devotion to letter writing and took up her pen with purpose. Paul was also at loose ends and a little desperate. What was to become of him, a single, middle-aged man with no career to speak of, living in a basement apartment in Washington, working somewhat reluctantly for the State Department? Her letters to him were upbeat and flirtatious; she regaled him with news of her intellectual self-improvement. She subscribed to the *Washington Post* and the *New York Times,* and devoured books on psychology, philosophy, and semantics. She

---

* Yes, human poo.

dutifully read Henry Miller, after Paul's recommendation, and wrote that she found his work to contain too many stiff pricks.

Julia, knowing that Paul's mother had been a terrific cook, began taking cooking lessons from two old English ladies in Beverly Hills, who specialized in pancakes. She was a terrible cook and regaled Paul with stories of her disasters, including the time she blew up a duck in the oven. Their talk of food and eating slid into sly confessions of wanting to eat each other, and Julia, on the whim of her life, invited him to come to Pasadena to see if what they both suspected was true: They were meant for each other.

Rule ^{No.} 5:

All You Need Is a Kitchen
and a Bedroom

❧

We analyzed one another, and concluded that marriage and advancing age agreed with us.

They docked at Le Havre at daybreak and arrived in Rouen, the medieval capital of Normandy, in time for lunch. It was November 3, 1948. Paul consulted the Michelin Guide and settled upon Restaurant La Couronne, located in a medieval, low-ceilinged house not far from the square where Joan of Arc was put to death. Someone else might have found the proximity of an execution site unnerving, but to Julia it was *history,* something they simply didn't have in California.

Inside, the place was cozy and close, built during the fourteenth century, when even the tiny French were much tinier. Julia had never felt more like a California hayseed, twice the size of everyone else, awkward in her American clothes, unable to speak French despite her many years of schooling.

The simple meal that changed Julia's life, and eventually the face of cooking in America:

six oysters served on the half shell, with *pain de seigle,* French rye bread

beurre d'Isigny, creamy unsalted French table butter*

the legendary sole meunière

green salad with vinaigrette

a baguette

fromage blanc, i.e., a really nice cheese plate

a cup of filtered coffee

With the exception of the oysters,† I've eaten a version of this meal about eight hundred times. I've ordered sole meunière in restaurants the world over (New York) and make it perhaps every other month at home with some not-cheap Dover sole from Whole Paycheck.

---

* So delicious it gets its own mention in *My Life in France,* and rightly so.

† Once, not long after my mother died and my father had moved to Newport Beach, California, we went to a nice restaurant overlooking the ocean. I can't remember the occasion, but I do remember that we slurped down our oysters, and then wound up in the ER a few hours later, where we each had our stomach pumped. That was the end of oysters for me.

Paul had come to adore the woman he once admired for having resigned herself to her old-maid status. He loved her for her stamina, competence, brains, guts, and good humor. What I love most about her, which is to say envy, was her ability to be enraptured by a piece of nicely cooked fish. In descriptions of that lunch in Rouen much is made of the buttery, succulent splendor of that sole, but her world was unmade by so much more. It was the medieval restaurant with the white walls and the low brown beams, the fire blazing in the fireplace with a chicken turning upon a spit, the attentive waiter with whom her beloved spoke his immaculate French, the care with which the meal was served, the Pouilly-Fumé (wine at lunch!). It was the whole French megillah. Years later, when Julia was famous she would often receive letters from people who asked not simply how they might learn to cook. They already knew the answer: They owned her cookbooks, but they were yearning to know how they might become passionate about it. She always answered the same thing: Go to France and eat.

Once I stumbled upon this in my research—that not only did other people understand that what was singular about Julia was not her recipes, per se, but her passion for perfecting them, and that the solution for self-infecting oneself with such passion lay in going to France and eating—I called my friend Kathy, the only person on earth who would understand the need to go to Paris and rent an apartment in Julia's old neighborhood and walk the streets that Julia walked and frequent the markets

Julia frequented, in an effort to re-create the *je ne sais quoi* that transformed Julia Child into *Julia*.

Kathy lives in San Francisco, and one weekend I flew from Portland to celebrate my birthday and powwow about our upcoming pilgrimage. Kathy spent eight hours and about $200 making what she called Julia's Bouillia, Julia's monster bouillabaisse. Julia had more than a few showstoppers, and her bouillabaisse was one of them. ". . . remember it originated as a simple, Mediterranean fisherman's soup, made from the day's catch or its unsalable leftovers," Julia reminds us in *Mastering*. The dish itself is ancient, having been brought to Marseille in 600 BC or thereabouts by Greek sailors.

Kathy is one of the few people I know who cooks from *Mastering* on a regular basis and doesn't view it as a beloved relic from an earlier time. She's undaunted by the multipaged mega-recipes that require you to flip back and forth between the earlier page that lists the eighteen steps required to properly sauté an onion and the page that lists the showstopper recipe at hand. Kathy is also not afflicted with tortured ambivalence, nor does she share my personal culinary algebra that the longer something takes to cook, the better it should taste—that for example, if a dish takes six hours to prepare, it should taste thirty-six times better than does my high-quality all-beef frank cooked over a gas burner and dipped in a jar of Grey Poupon. I don't believe this is possible, whereas Kathy doesn't care whether it's possible. Like this:

Graph of Personal Culinary Algebra

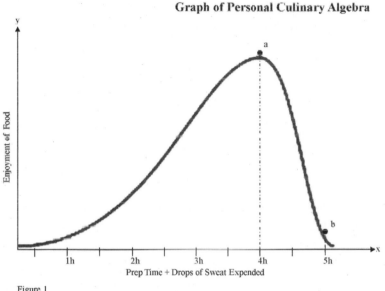

Figure 1

The longer you spend preparing a meal, the better it tastes... until you take too long and then no matter how good the food is, you're exhausted, starving, irritable, and incapable of enjoying anything.

(a) Moans of Ecstasy
(b) Cries of Despair

In fairness, I should say that Kathy's version of Julia's Bouillia, in which she uses the less-expensive Trader Joe's flash-frozen cod and mahi-mahi for the fish soup base, and fresh red snapper, cod, and clams for the bouillabaisse proper is worth all the work, and when we ate it that night in her San Francisco apartment—with

its dazzling view of the East Bay and a wedge of downtown*—
served with a green salad, a good baguette, and some Napa Valley
pinot grigio, I knew without a doubt that the meal would have
had the Julia bon appétit seal of approval.

ALL YOU NEED IS A KITCHEN, AND NOT A VERY GOOD ONE
Earlier in the afternoon, while Kathy stood at the stove in her
galley kitchen and stirred, I went online and found a perfect
Paris apartment for us to rent in the 7th arrondissement, a few
blocks west of Julia and Paul's apartment on rue de l'Université.
Our primary concern was renting a place that had a kitchen big
enough for both of us to stand in at the same time, and maybe a
window, although if it was impossibly cramped and dingy, that
would be okay too, since Julia's kitchen was appalling, and it did
nothing to dampen her spirit. It was to kitchens what a Porta-
Potty at a construction site is to the en-suite master bath at the
Four Seasons.

It was the only room on the third floor, occupied almost
exclusively by a mammoth coal-heated stove that went cold
every time there was a coal shortage, which happened not infre-
quently in postwar Paris; it had a separate tiny, two-burner con-
traption that came up to Julia's thigh, a weensy box oven in
which you could bake a cupcake, and a sink that ran only cold
water, and whose pipes froze a half dozen times every winter.

---

* Also Candlestick Park. When the Giants are playing at home you can watch the fireworks
over the stadium both in real time and two seconds later on TV.

The point is that Julia's first important kitchen was one step above a campfire in front of a cave, but that did nothing to dampen her enthusiasm for learning to cook. Nor did the half-assed situation at Le Cordon Bleu, where she enrolled in 1949, after a short, failed attempt to become a hat maker.* Due to the war and bad management, the once-great cooking school was down at the heels, lacking both basic equipment and ingredients. Often, if they ran out of something during class, someone would be sent out to the market to purchase some more with his or her own money. Also, Julia was in a class with eleven former servicemen who, taking advantage of the G.I. bill, hoped to learn how to cook well enough to return to the States and open a diner, or a snack bar at their local bowling alley.

None of it mattered; Julia was ecstatic. "How magnificent to find my life's calling at last," she said. She was thirty-eight years old.

To me, this is one of Julia's finest qualities: her ability not just to make do but to excel, even in god-awful circumstances. She never needed anything to be perfect or easy; in fact, I suspect she preferred the difficulty that comes with having to muddle through.

Thus, it wasn't necessary for Kathy and me to rent an apartment with a fine kitchen; just an all-right kitchen would do. And we found one, in a one-bedroom apartment on the rue de l'Exposition, above a hair salon called Confidence. Could there be a better omen?

---

* One wonders how our relationship to cooking would be different if Julia Child had not had the good sense to get out of millinery.

Our apartment was predictably less spacious than the pictures on the Internet rental site suggested, and the layout was curious, with the bathroom just inside the front door, then a long hallway that opened out into the bedroom on the right, and the sitting room and kitchen to the left. Thomas, the upbeat English speaker sent by the rental agency, showed us how everything worked and pressed both Kathy and me to practice locking and unlocking the finicky front door; not a minute after he left, we perused the kitchen. There was a nice L-shaped counter, cupboards filled with IKEA plates and cups, a deep sink, and a stove top. Where the oven should have been, there was a clothes washer.

I opened the washing machine and stuck my head inside, just in case to our jet-lagged American eyes it only looked like a clothes washer but was really a sleek, modern European oven, perhaps manufactured in Scandinavia.

Tant pis! we thought with what we hoped was Julian esprit, remembering her cruddy, cold-water kitchen (but at least she had an oven, however small) and putting a positive spin on her comment in *Mastering* regarding kitchen equipment: "Theoretically a good cook should be able to perform under any circumstance, but cooking is much easier, pleasanter and more efficient if you have the right tools." That would be us: *performing under any circumstances.*

In following Julia's advice to go to France to eat, we didn't think it would be necessary to cook strictly from *Mastering*. Not only has Julie Powell already scaled that particular mountain, but if I'm to be honest, I must admit that when my tortured on-again, off-again love affair with cooking is on, I prefer Julia's less-Frenchcentric *The Way to Cook,* which I dragged along in my suitcase, along with my other favorite, *From Julia Child's Kitchen,* published in 1975.*

In the spirit of Julia, we decided not to fret about our lack of an oven and skipped over to rue Cler, only a few blocks away, to shop for dinner. Julia preferred patronizing her neighborhood market around the corner from Roo de Loo on the rue de Bourgogne, but occasionally she wandered over to cobblestoned rue Cler, where anything you might want to eat or cook can be found; there's a green grocer, with fruits and vegetables trucked in before dawn from local farms, a fromagerie you can smell from down the block, a poissonnerie, a charcuterie, a boulangerie, a patisserie,† and a small FranPrix grocery store, where you can buy an excellent three-euro bottle of Chardonnay, which we did that afternoon, and every afternoon thereafter because you can never go wrong having a three-euro bottle of Chardonnay on hand.

---

* I own the original 1975 edition, which sports a picture of Julia on the cover wearing a snazzy blue and white floral Qiana disco shirt, and a terrific, literary description beneath the title: "With hundreds of delicious recipes—her own personal variations of the French classics as well as a multitude of new dishes using everyday foods (soups, stews, vegetables, beans, pasta, an American Fish Chowder, the Perfect Roast Turkey)—here is Julia Child, with her incomparable gift for explaining the whys and wherefores of cooking, delighting you with her own experiences, and sharing her findings about everything in the kitchen from microwaves and magic mixers to meat cuts and weeping meringues." *Weeping meringues.*

† In France it is believed that if you can bake bread, you cannot possibly make pastries, and vice versa. It's one or the other.

❧

Julia, for all her pragmatism, was also a great romantic, and she believed that you could learn both French and the secret to living well by shopping for food in France, which requires one to trade quips with the green grocer, absorb the philosophy of the butcher, and listen sympathetically to the woes of Madame from whom you buy your daily baguette. She believed this even though when she first arrived in Paris her French was wretched; it got worse before it got better. It was murder for such an extrovert as Julia, and after enduring a Thanksgiving party hosted by Mrs. Paul Mowrer (better known as Hadley, Ernest Hemingway's first wife, with whom Paul had been acquainted when he lived in Paris in the 1920s), where her incomprehensible French required her to remain more or less mute, she signed up at Berlitz, engaged the help of her first French friend, Hélène Baltrusaitis,* and threw herself and her "honking consonants" on everyone she met.

She was determined to become fluent in the language of her beloved Paris—practically impossible, by the way, even for the French—and so every day she dutifully went out into the streets and talked and talked and talked, which meant that every day, for a very long time, she subjected herself to humiliating encounter after humiliating encounter with mechanics (the Blue Flash,

---

* A vivacious Parisian married to a famous Lithuanian art historian and cultural advisor to the American Embassy, where Paul worked.

the station wagon they'd shipped from the States, was making a weird noise), bureaucrats (in order to establish residency she needed to fill out reams of paperwork), postal workers (how do you mail a letter?), and, of course, shop people. The French are among the only people on earth who despise you on principle for not speaking their language perfectly, and Julia put herself in the way of them every day. Julia Child could "bring out the best in a polecat," as Paul once said of his warm and friendly wife. I don't even have to know what polecats are to know that they are nicer and less judgmental than your average Parisian.

The genuine extent of my French is this: Bonjour, Madame!

Technically, of course, I speak more French than this, but this is the limit of what I can speak with élan, or anything resembling authority. In France, it's customary to say Bonjour, M'dame or Bonjour, M'sieur whenever you enter a shop.* To enter and say anything else is considered the height of rudeness. I can *Bonjour, Madame* with the best of them. I can *Bonjour, Madame* with the conviction of a third-generation concierge. But that's the end of it. If the M'dame or M'sieur replies with anything other than *Bonjour M'dame*, I've got nothing. What's worse, I'm aware that the quality of my *Bonjour, Madame* is so fine—I've mastered the perfect high-pitched, slightly querulous tone, the almost but not quite silent first "a" in Madame, the general air of having bonjoured a million madames in my time—I am bound to be confused with a near-native speaker.

---

* I'm even unclear about this. A few friends who've lived in Paris insist it's actually Bonjour, m'sieurs dames, a sort of contraction of the older, more formal Bonjour Messieurs, Mesdames.

Or if not a near-native speaker, at least not an American. I feel both shame and guilt about this predicament; shame because given the number of years of French I studied in school (six), and the number of times I've been to France (also six), you think I'd be able to do better. Guilt, because every time I *Bonjour, Madame* someone, I'm flying under the flag of false fluency.

As Kathy and I approached our first shop, it started to rain. We had neither hoods nor umbrellas. The five-hour energy drink I'd downed in the cab on the way from the airport was many hours ago. I tried to summon the spirit of Julia in her most polecat-charming mood, but it did nothing to alleviate the basic dread I always felt upon entering a shop in Paris, further complicated now, since I was on a pilgrimage, with the despair at never being able to speak enough French to learn Julia's secret to living well. Surely Julia didn't mean the secret to living well was being thought an imbecile by every French person you met, did she?

We entered the green grocer first and I ardently greeted the only person who looked as if he worked there, a kid of perhaps sixteen wearing a white apron and a knit cap. He looked at us as if he wasn't quite sure we were talking to him. When we brought our basket to the register and I *Bonjour, M'sieured* him again, he said, "Hey," or something that sounded like "Hey." The one thing he did not say was *Bonjour, Mesdames*. I looked at him again and pegged him as the American pop culture–loving son of, perhaps, an Algerian owner. One thing he wasn't was a disapproving Parisian matron (not to worry, she was manning the counter over at the fromagerie).

"Tiens, il pleut!" I blurted out. (Hey look, it's raining.)
"Il fait froid, aussi," he said. (It's cold, too.)
"Merci beaucoup! Tu es, I mean, vous êtes, vous êtes si bon!"
I pretty much shrieked. (Thank you! You are very kind!)

Had I been able to continue my thought, "I am grateful that
you have resisted treating me like a complete imbecile!" I would
have, but I settled for smiling and dipping my head like a horse
about to dig into some fresh alfalfa.

The relief I felt was all out of proportion to this simple
exchange, and I had a sudden inkling, trudging home in the
drizzle along the rue de Grenelle, that this may have been Julia's
secret. Whether she knew it or not—and given her innate optimism it's doubtful she gave it a thought—her successful conversations with the shopkeepers, bureaucrats, waiters, tobacconists,
and more mechanics (the Blue Flash was now making yet
another weird noise) on whom she practiced her French were
many times more encouraging and glad-making than the disas-
trous ones. She possessed the type of personality that set much
more store by the good than by the bad. Good experiences were
that much more good than bad experiences were bad. It was
not simply a matter of refusing to dwell on the bad; the good
was just so much better, so much more energy infusing, inspirational, and satisfying, it simply drew more attention to itself.
The bad, like the promises we make to see more of people we
don't really like, falls away, forgotten.

I recently purchased and devoured a book called *The Anti-
dote: Happiness for People Who Can't Stand Positive Thinking,*

which tells you everything you need to know about my aptitude for unbridled optimism. But this realization, that one good
exchange was worth, say, a dozen discouraging ones, was something I could get behind, in part because there are no mental
gymnastics involved in trying to find a way to transform the bad
into the good, the fallback position of most knee-jerk positive
thinkers.

Back at the apartment, we made omelets and *Pommes de
Terre Sautées à la Catalane* (potatoes sautéed with onions and
peppers), basically, a fancy breakfast dinner. While Kathy cut
the potatoes and failed to fret in a very Julia manner that we'd
forgotten to get lardons,* I further inspected the kitchen and
took stock of our *batterie de cuisine*: We were without a whisk,
a cutting board, measuring spoons, measuring cups, or a cheese
grater. All of these items we could easily purchase and leave for
the next renter. But what to do about the lack of an oven? Over
our cheese course—we sprang for a wedge of Brie de Meaux at
the fromagerie—Kathy left a message for Marcelline, the one
person we knew in Paris well enough to barge in on and com-
mandeer her oven.

While waiting to hear back from Marcelline, we fell into a
routine. In the morning we brewed coffee in our unromantic,
rental apartment Krups coffeemaker, and while one of us ran
to the corner boulangerie (croissant for me, pain au raisin for

---

* The cubes or strips of pork belly that show up in a lot of Julia's recipes; they give butter a run
for its money.

Kathy), the other would start planning a dinner that could be adapted to the stove top,* which then took the rest of the day to shop for and prepare.

The day we settled on a relatively simple dish of *Filet de Poisson Pochés au Vin Blanc* (fish filets poached in white wine) with *Sauce Hollandaise,* we spent most of it in search of wax paper, which Julia, who is lax when it comes to certain things, insisted we use to cover the fish while it simmered; aluminum foil apparently discolors the wine. This sort of attention to detail is what helped Julia make her name, but it plunged Kathy and me into a Kafkaesque search for *papier paraffiné.* From Fran-Prix to MonoPrix to Biomonde, no wax paper. I'm sure we were pronouncing it wrong. The word paraffiné in the wrong mouth (mine) might sound, I don't know, like *par a fini,* which means "finished by." *Bonjour, Madame, do you have any paper finished by?* Kathy's French is moderately better than mine, but it didn't seem to matter. No one in Paris had any paper finished by. We decided we could make do with a piece of buttered notebook paper, of which we had plenty.

Not a moment after we checked wax paper off our list, we were faced with what to substitute for the "white wine fish stock made from heads, bones and trimmings."

This is as good a place as any to discuss Julia's money, which we tend to lose sight of in the face of her unflappable can do,

---

* We figured out pretty quickly that Julia stuck a lot of stuff in the oven that could easily simmer on the stove.

DIY spirit. Despite that generous inheritance, Julia was always frugal. When she and Paul were married, they resolved to live on his civil service salary, which they managed to do by economizing on furnishings for their various rental apartments first in Paris; then Marseille; Plattsdorf, Germany; and Oslo. You never hear about Julia splurging on a Persian silk rug or a Dior dress,* nor did Pulia, as they liked to call themselves, ever say, as far as we know, "This cold Parisian fog is simply too much to bear, we need a week in Cancun."

What they did spend her money on was groceries, eating out, and outfitting Julia with the most spectacular *batterie de cuisine* in Paris, smaller only than that of E. Dehillerin, the famous kitchen supply store on the rue Coquillière, near the Louvre, where she would often buy so many copper pots, aluminum pans, casseroles, molds, grinders, graters, choppers, strainers, bowls, funnels, egg rings and separators, boning knives, bread knives, paring knives, cleavers, and whisks, she would have to make two trips in the Blue Flash.

When Julia wasn't cooking at home, she and Paul worked their way through the *Guide Michelin*. They preferred two-star restaurants, where they could get a meal for about five dollars. Michaud became their regular haunt for a while—Julia adored the sole meunière, and the bustling friendly proprietress, who at four feet three was a full two feet shorter—and they also loved

---

* Not that anything in Paris would fit her. Nothing in Paris fits an average-size American, much less a woman of Julia's stature.

Le Grand Véfour, one of Paris's oldest restaurants, where they ate scallops and duck, and spied the writer Colette in the corner, tucking into a plate of sausages.

It pains me to be the fun-killer, but I feel compelled to point out what most first worlders of a certain economic class who are devoted to eating well, however we individually define it, prefer not to think about: Food can be expensive. And I'm not talking about the meals at the world's lofty food shrines, the $500 prix-fixe menu at Masa in New York or Alain Ducasse au Plaza Athénée in Paris, or any of the other fine-dining restaurants where dinner for two is a month's mortgage. I mean if, for example, you're with a friend in Paris and you're trying to cook in the manner of Julia Child and want to make a nice white wine fish stock with bones, heads, and trimmings. I have no doubt that there is a shop somewhere in Paris where you can purchase a fish carcass, or that somewhere there was a jovial, tolerant fishmonger who would be enchanted by our mission, not that we could explain it in French, and for a euro or two sell us some bones, heads, and trimmings, but all we could think of at the moment was that we would have to purchase a few whole fish (in addition to the filets) from which to make the stock, and even though we had saved money by substituting buttered notebook paper for wax paper, we suddenly feared for our budget.

Kathy and I have known each other since the Reagan administration. We were roommates when John Lennon was shot. For a time, just after we graduated from film school, we spent a half dozen years collaborating on the same number of genius screenplays that, of course, went nowhere. We've been there for each other through love affairs, marriages, births, divorces: Our now-twentysomething children have known one another since they were born. Our long history has paved the way for like-minded thinking a lot of the time, and when we stood in the middle of the MonoPrix on the rue de Rennes, contemplating the fish stock dilemma, we were reminded of the stupendous Julia Bouillia Kathy had so lovingly labored over months earlier; even with the cheapo Trader Joe's flash-frozen fish, that bouillabaisse set us back $200.

One of Julia's most basic, enduring lessons is the layering of flavors, and every one of those layers, when made with the finest ingredients, costs money. But Julia, despite her Pasadena privilege, was also a woman of great common sense and empathy. She never wanted the inability to find or afford the right ingredients to trip up a home cook; she always offered alternatives. Indeed, later in her career she would be mocked and snubbed by foodies of every stripe for daring to suggest a meal might be tasty using a canned anything. Even though her recipes are maddeningly precise and have a perverse number of steps, she always suggests an alternative that, while not perfect, will do just fine. In our case, the substitution for the white wine fish stock was white wine, vermouth, and *jus de palourdes* (clam juice).

Trying to find clam juice was the same business as with the wax paper. The stores we tried either didn't stock it or the notoriously blasé Parisian clerks weren't interested in trying to understand what we wanted. We wound up settling for boxed vegetable broth.

We lugged our groceries back to rue de l'Exposition in the sideways rain. Once at the apartment, we realized we'd forgotten to purchase a whisk, and you simply can't make *Sauce Hollandaise* without a whisk. So we switched to *Sauce à la Parisienne,* a cream and egg sauce made with a flour and butter roux from the fish-poaching liquid, which is not as flavorful as a *Sauce Hollandaise* but much sturdier and more difficult to ruin. We'd left our apartment just after breakfast and now it was late afternoon. I had a roaring headache and needed water. Forget the mystery about why French women don't get fat: How do they stride around Paris without collapsing on the cobblestones from dehydration? There are no drinking fountains in the city, and you'll spot a unicorn before you'll see a French woman stopping on the street to take a swig from a water bottle.

In the apartment next door, our neighbor was shrieking either to someone on the phone, or to someone in her apartment who was bound and gagged. The neighbor, who we hadn't yet seen, started shouting every morning at 7:00 a.m. and shouted on and off all day long. She didn't merely raise her voice; it was the kind of hysterical raging that generally precedes lunging at someone. She wasn't yelling in French, or any language we recognized. The Romanian Embassy was across the street. Perhaps it was Romanian?

Reader, did I mention that our apartment was mere steps away from rue Saint-Dominique, and thus some terrific restaurants? There was La Fontaine de Mars, where Michelle Obama ate, and a little farther down the street, the little fiefdom of Christian Constant, with his trio of well-reviewed restaurants: the casual Le Café Constant, the formal (and out of our price range) Le Violon d'Ingres, and the hip Les Cocottes.* Why am I mentioning this?

Because we could have gone out to eat. Because I'm the kind of person who memorized something Tim Kreider wrote in an op-ed called "The Busy Trap" for the *New York Times*: "The Puritans turned work into a virtue, evidently forgetting that God invented it as a punishment." Because we were in Paris, and trying to cook this stupid fish was Too. Much. Work. Did Julia really think this was fun? She was insane.

By the time we finally set about poaching the fish, in a skillet and not the suggested baking dish, because, as you know, we were ovenless American cooks, I was losing the will. Kathy was not losing the will. Kathy had uncorked the wine and was merrily chopping the shallots and floating various theories about the mental state of the screaming neighbor.

I leaned out the window and watched while a gaggle of gorgeous young Romanians in skinny jeans and roguishly knotted scarves left the embassy. It occurred to me that in our eagerness

---

* A cocotte is a small cast-iron casserole, in which French comfort food is served. The chicken fricassee is supposed to be swoonworthy.

to experience French food the way Julia did when she was learning to cook, we forgot one major ingredient, for which there
was no substitution: Paul. Paul! Julia was practically a newlywed
when she moved to Paris. She was cooking for Paul, the love of
her life, and Kathy and I were cooking for the heck of it. True
food people like to say that to be a great chef, or even merely
a good one, you must cook with love. It feels churlish to think
too deeply about what this means, but I believe my tortured
ambivalence gives me license. Are they talking about love for the
people for whom you're cooking? Love of the art and discipline
required? Love of ingredients?* Or, to paraphrase Bill Buford,
are the people who cook with love cooking in order to be loved?
It hardly matters when we're talking about Julia Child, because
she cooked with every kind of cooking love out there.

ALL YOU NEED IS TO *NEED* THE BEDROOM†
"If we could just have the kitchen and the bedroom, that would
be all we need," Julia said, wistfully, to Ruth Reichl, who was
interviewing her for the *Smithsonian* magazine, as her iconic
kitchen was being packed up for its trip to Washington D.C.,
where it would be on display at the National Museum of American History. The year was 2001; Julia was eighty-nine and a
widow. Paul had died seven years earlier, in 1994.

---

* Images of Alice Waters stroking a stalk of celery and fondling a lemon come to mind.

† In other words, putting out has got to be a priority.

In her piece Reichl commented that even though Paul had been gone for so long, he remained so present for Julia, and it felt, a little eerily, as if he would walk through the door at any minute.

Admirers of Julia also tend to admire the forty-eight-year-long love affair that was her marriage to Paul Child. I've been married and divorced and have lived with Jerrod, my beloved, for a dozen years and prefer it that way, so I'm either the perfect person or the worst person to parse what made the Childs' marriage work so well that Julia, at nearly ninety, was still thinking about her long-gone love in terms of the pleasures of the bedroom. The desire—and ability—to see your partner in a sexual light decade in, decade out, may be the only real requirement for a happy marriage, but in the event it really is more complicated than that, here are a few of Julia's other secrets.

Whatever you do, don't settle.

Over the past few years there have been a spate of hard-nosed books telling it like it is: If marriage is high on your adult To Do list, you should snag the first reasonably employed guy who doesn't live with his parents. No one and nothing is perfect, and holding out for someone on the order of Paul Child only puts you further down the road toward having to freeze your eggs or dabbling in animal hoarding.

Hooking your cart to someone you "love" because he res-
cues you from being single is a bad idea for so many reasons, but
the one that concerns us here is this: Had Julia said yes to rich,
boring Harrison Chandler—who was still interested in courting
her after the war, when the OSS was dissolved and Julia had
no choice but to return to Pasadena (now at the ripe old age
of thirty-three, an old maid in full) to care for her crotchety,
right-wing father—she would have been settling, and she would
have been miserable. Chandler, a man of her class, who could
have given her a comfortable life and perhaps even children,
was not the man for her. Had she married him, most likely she
would have gone on to become a Pasadena society lady, active
at the local tennis club and in community theater, and maybe a
little too fond of mid-afternoon martinis. She would have lan-
guished, her genius never realized.

My feminist within would love to be able to make a case for
Julia's having discovered her singular gift for cooking, teaching,
"cookery-bookery," as she called it, and her genius level TVQ,
on her own, but it's impossible. Paul was the final and mostim-
portant piece of Julia's self-actualization. It's not a stretch to say
he gave her herself, and Julia was well aware of it. She had no
doubt that without Paul she would have failed to find her life's
purpose and passion.

Paul did much more than introduce Julia to the glories
of Paris. She may have had the fancy college degree, but Paul

possessed the genuine love of learning. He taught Julia to love Balzac, which she read in the original French, and while she made dinner he'd often read to her.* She was well aware of the way in which Paul had and was schooling her. In a letter to Avis she wrote, vis-à-vis her intellectual rigor, "except for La Cuisine, I find I have to push myself to build up a thirst for how the atomic bomb works, or a study of Buddhism, etc."

Be prepared to dust off the pom-poms.
I'm as guilty as anyone of making perhaps too much about Paul's enrichment of Julia's life. Perhaps it's because *she* never failed to give him credit. But in her continuous praise and expression of gratitude, as constant as a heartbeat, we see what she gave him: full-time access to her *joie de vivre*, sense of humor, and optimism.

For Paul, it must be said, could be a sourpuss. When they met, he was going through a full-fledged middle-age crisis, and he despaired that he had done so many interesting things in his life but had nothing to show for it. He was conflicted about his art, his relationship with Charlie, his twin, who he felt was the picture of success, and his various Foreign Service jobs, where he felt underappreciated.

---

* A favorite was the "light" *Boswell in Holland.*

Paul was more like an average person, going about his life in a light drizzle of dissatisfaction, with a few sun breaks of joy. But Julia shored him up, buoyed his spirits, endlessly championed what was great about him, and ignored the other stuff.

Please appreciate the word endlessly.

Part of the secret of their great marriage—or any great marriage—is shoring up the other guy, regardless. You are always not simply on his (or her) team, you're his head cheerleader. Julia had Paul's back in a way no one else did, not even his twin brother. Even when they were going through the "or for worse" part of the vows, Julia was devoted to doing everything she could to move them into "the better."

Before Paul retired in 1961, the same year *Mastering* was published, and the unlikely switcheroo occurred, where he devoted his life to her career, Julia was the perfect Foreign Service man's wife, attending countless cocktail parties, dinners, receptions, and cultural exhibits on her husband's arm; hosting luncheons and dinners—sometimes every evening, depending on which mucky-muck was in town; and making an effort always to be positive, charming, and full of laughs. Once, she returned home from her morning shopping around 11:30 a.m., intending to cook all day, and had a message from her husband that he was bringing home members of the visiting U.S. Fencing Team for lunch. Every dish in the place was dirty, the beds were unmade, books and papers were strewn around the living room, and clouds of cat hair scudded around the baseboards. She tidied up and put up a pot of *Soupe de Pistou* without a syllable of complaint.

Can you imagine doing all this for someone you'd settled for? He better damn well be the love of your life.

Practice husbandcentricity.

In fairness to all of us with children, Julia was able to tend to Paul the way she did because they didn't have children, only a cat, Minou. Thus, her attention was divided only between her work and her man, not, like so many of us, between our work, our man, and the impossible demands of contemporary hothouse parenting.

This may seem obvious, but if you want to have a successful, world-class marriage, you need to pay attention, and I mean a lot of attention, to your spouse. I know not one, not two, but *three* grown men who confessed to having shed a tear during the movie *Avatar*. All of them cited having been wrecked by the Navi greeting *"Oel ngati kame"* ("I see you.")* It could be because the greeting was delivered mostly by Neytiri, the hot Navi chick played by Zoe Saldana, or because these guys, all husbands and fathers of young children, felt less like men and lovers and more like the unpaid nanny. Nothing bums out the man of the house more than being the object of your lust and

---

* In this created-for-the-movie language, there are two words for "to see." *Tse'a* means to see with your eyes; *kame,* to see with your heart, to "understand."

adoration, only to be transformed overnight into a pair of extra hands once the baby is born.

When people say marriage takes work, this is the work they mean, taking the time every single day to actually see the person you loved enough to marry. The best places to do this? The kitchen and the bedroom.

Rule №. 6:

To Be Happy, Work Hard

⚜

There is so much that has been written, by people so much more professional than I, that I wonder what in the hell I am presuming to do, anyway.

POSTWAR PARIS WASN'T ALL CRÊPES SUZETTES AND LADIES SWANN-
ing around in nip-waisted dresses. Not surprisingly, we have the
movies to blame for this impression. Pretty much every American movie set during the early 1950s in Paris achieves its historic
magic by putting the actors in fedoras and parking a few beautiful old Peugeots on the street and calling it authentic, which it
was, minus the shell shock and pieces of cardboard people were
still lashing to their feet in place of shoes. During the first years
Paul and Julia lived there, there were endless shortages; days
would pass without enough coal for the stove, so that preparing a simple lamb chop and a pan of peas was an ordeal. There

was a fierce drought in the summer of 1949; vegetable crops and vineyards were withered and wasted by September, causing a steep rise in produce prices. Then, just when Paris seemed to be regaining her mojo as a world-class city, the General Strikes of 1951* meant weeks without public transportation. Paul and Julia rose to the occasion, employing the Blue Flash to shuttle their friends and Paul's colleagues at the embassy wherever they needed to go.

But Julia was always at her best when she had to buck up and make do. Whether she was aware of it or not, a life of ease failed to bring out her best qualities. Difficult circumstances never seemed a reason not to do what you wanted to do, and after a few months at Le Cordon Bleu, with its own shortages of basic equipment and ingredients, cooking became the only thing Julia thought about, aside from Paul. Her days began at 6:30 a.m. and ended at midnight. She cooked in class all morning, returned to her Roo de Loo attic kitchen and cooked between classes, went back to Le Cordon Bleu in the afternoon, where she paid extra for special demonstrations, then came home in the evening to serve dinner and entertain. As we all know from *Julie & Julia,* most days she and Paul had a nooner.

The making of Julia Child is such an oft-told tale that it bears reminding ourselves that Julia's enthusiasm and commitment to cooking was a little bizarre. We tend to forget, I think, that she did not have a Julia Child to inspire her to scale the Everest that is *Pâté de Canard en Croûte.* Few women of her class

---

* It's a French tradition to always be striking about something.

in Paris did their own cooking. Most bourgeois Parisian households had live-in maids and at least a part-time cook. What Julia
was doing in the attic kitchen on the Roo do Loo was to her time
and place as a friend's architect husband who makes charcuterie*
is to ours: cool, but a little over the top. That the apartment
Kathy and I rented in one of the best zip codes in Paris didn't
have an oven proved that while the French revere *haute cuisine,*
everyday people aren't really expected to master cooking it.

When Julia wasn't cooking she attended luncheons and lec
tures at Le Cercle des Gourmettes, a ladies culinary club that
existed primarily because no women were allowed in Le Cercle
des Gourmets. In France, not only were men the only humans
who truly knew how to cook, but also they were, apparently, the
only ones who knew how to eat. Normally, Julia wasn't a fan of
all-female groups—perhaps she'd had enough after her all-girls
high school and college—but so eager was she to avail herself
of every culinary opportunity in Paris, she thought *Why not?*
Members were invited to show up at 10:00 a.m. on the days of
their luncheons, and Julia rarely missed the opportunity.

Around the same time, Julia met Simone Beck. Simca,† whose
"family" recipes she'd learned at the knee of the family's cook in
Normandy, had already published one slim book about prunes
and prune liquors, and when she and Julia became acquainted,

---

* His duck breast prosciutto with juniper berries and peppercorns, cured in the basement-
cum-meat-curing-cellar, is quite tasty.

† She was nicknamed after a popular make of car. The acronym stands for *Société Industrielle de
Mécanique et de Carrosserie Automobile.* The modern-day iteration would be a chic, yet thrifty
and eco-aware, friend named Prius.

she was working on another book with Louisette Bertholle, translating French recipes for an American audience. The first draft had been rejected by the original American publisher, who felt it was too dry, and lacking in any background or instruction in French attitudes about food and cooking. They needed an American who understood the degree to which American cooks were clueless when it came to *La Cuisine,* and Julia agreed to see what she could do in order to make the book more accessible, i.e., create the "blah-blah" (Louisette's term for the friendly background explanations Americans seemed to require).

Meanwhile, the three also hatched a plan to give cooking lessons to Americans. They named themselves L'Ecole des Trois Gourmandes, Paul designed their stylish badges (the same one Julia faithfully wore on *The French Chef),* and they corralled three students for their first class. They were in business!

I must pause here for a side note: How on earth did three wealthy women who grew up in households with at least one live-in cook come to focus on the humble needs of middle-class women like my mother, who was required by the middle-class mores of her day to produce breakfast, lunch, and dinner seven days a week, three-hundred-sixty-five days a year? Simca had the classic French aristocratic upbringing, including the requisite servants and English nannies, while Julia experienced the more rustic Southern California version of same. Even Avis DeVoto, Julia's pen pal and confidant, herself an avid cook, could pursue her culinary passion because a maid came in three days a week. Mary would come at 10:00 a.m., clean the house, and serve dinner at six-thirty, "a perfectly horrible hour," Avis once groused. Furthermore, Louisette, the weak link in the collaboration, was unable to share Julia and Simca's fierce time-consuming obsession, because her impending divorce and financial instability impelled her to think about something other than writing a cookbook. She had the usual messy life, in other words.

Even the now infamous rallying cry from the introduction to *Mastering*—"This is a book for the servantless American cook who can be unconcerned on occasion with budgets, waistlines, time schedules, children's meals, the parent–chauffeur–den mother syndrome or anything else which might interfere with the enjoyment of producing something wonderful to eat"—presumes that the "occasion" during which a regular housewife and mother can be "unconcerned" with all of those tasks at once is more frequent than the reality, which was close to never.

And yet, they had to address their book to someone, and the American "housewife-chauffeur," who read women's magazines and whose highest culinary aspirations consisted of entering the Pillsbury Bake-Off,* must have seemed as good a person as any. What could they possibly have known of the servantless American cook? Other than, like the savages in deepest Africa who were the object of Christian missionary zeal, she was in desperate need of enlightenment.

---

* The first Grand National Recipe and Baking Contest was held at New York's Waldorf Astoria and won by Theodora Smafield for her No-Knead Water-Rising Twists. Little did Theodora know that a dozen years later she would be struggling with the concept of *en croûte*.

Julia's true motives might be that of the natural-born educator that she proved to be, or maybe something more complicated—there but for the grace of Paul Child go I—but in any case she gets a pass, in part because we adore her beyond all reason, and also because she never asked anyone to do anything that she hadn't done at least a hundred times herself.

For the next eight years, give or take, Julia hurled herself into what she called "cookery-bookery." There is no other appropriate noun. She and Simca (and sometimes Louisette) cooked and tasted and re-cooked and re-tasted and re-re-cooked and re-re-tasted enough recipes to comprise a first-draft manuscript of more than five hundred pages—and this covered only soups and poultry. They worked with the zeal of law school students determined to graduate at the top of their class, cooking and writing upwards of eighty hours a week.

Simca and Julia grew to love each other like sisters. Theirs was a relationship of deep devotion interrupted by the occasional homicidal fantasy. Simca's bursts of irrationality combined with her general lack of tact and attention to details tried the endless patience of the organized, methodical Julia.

Their need for each other was like something out of an O. Henry story: Without Simca, Julia would not have access to the hundreds of authentic French recipes that only Simca—or someone like her—could provide; and without Julia, Simca had no access to an American sensibility that could make sense of her classic, complex, never-before-deconstructed dishes.

Julia dubbed Simca *La Super-Française*, and she was, indeed, one of those energetic, exacting, relentless European women who, after a while, can drive even someone as sunny and diplomatic as Julia Child around the bend. One of the things that irritated Julia beyond measure, aside from Simca's habit of sputtering "But it's not French!" when there was some aspect of a recipe of which she disapproved for no reason that she could articulate, was that, like almost all French women of a certain age, she deferred to men.

Over the eight years it took to complete the book, they prepared, adjusted, tasted, and re-tasted hundreds if not thousands of recipes, and yet, if they found themselves at odds over say, a tomato sauce in which Julia experimented by adding green peppers or carrots, Simca would insist upon deferring to some doddering one-star male chef to settle the matter, rather than relying on their own findings. This drove Julia exceptionally mad, since behind every *Guide Michelin* chef there was a woman, usually a precious, four foot five, cataract-ridden old granny from whom he'd filched his best recipes.

Julia was fortunate in carrying the genes for both Yankee self-reliance and the American West pioneering spirit, and she believed completely in their own "operational proof," a term she'd picked up from Paul, who learned it from his physicist father. She tried to impose her American character on Simca, encouraging her to stick up for herself and to trust her own experience.

MASTERING THE ART OF FINDING YOURSELF THROUGH AN IMPOSSIBLY LONG AND SEEMINGLY INSURMOUNTABLE PROJECT OF UNKNOWN VALUE

The general wisdom about following your bliss suggests that most likely you'll be happy pursuing a field for which you have a natural aptitude, but Julia Child wasn't a natural cook, nor for a long time was she even a good cook. It's an imaginative exercise to see past the formidable expert she became, to imagine her in her cold Paris apartment, bent over her typewriter, struggling to write the recipes that would one day comprise *Mastering,* which for years she called her "scratches."

One of the reasons she felt the need to devote an entire morning to writing a recipe for cooking lobster, as a way of documenting exactly what needed to be done, step by step, was so that she could follow that particular trail back into the woods the next time she wanted to make it. She needed to have a perfect, highly detailed recipe because she feared she lacked perfect culinary pitch. Had she been a more instinctive, "natural" cook, she might have felt less compelled to parse each recipe, to tackle each one as though getting it right were a matter of life and death. The recipes are so infamously long because Julia herself required such details.

Evidence of her obsession, and the ecstasy it produced, would fill an entire book, and did. Page after page of *As Always, Julia: The Letters of Julia Child and Avis DeVoto* is filled with lengthy passages attesting to Julia's near-manic joy about food: eating it, cooking it, and everything associated with it: "We also ran into a beautiful

Bordeaux 1929, that is just perfectly matured, and is everything one reads about that a wonderful Bordeaux should be but rarely tastes. It is really something to swoon over, the wonderful rich exciting bouquet, that excitement as it fills the mouth . . . I'm swooning over the typewriter just at the thought of them."

In 1952, while Julia was still hoping, somehow, to make a career around cooking, she wrote a fan letter to a journalist and historian named Bernard DeVoto in response to a piece he'd written in *Harper's Magazine* bemoaning the mediocre stainless-steel knives found in most American kitchens. So grateful was Julia that someone had brought this egregious problem to light, she sent along a "nice little French model" from her *batterie de cuisine*.

Avis DeVoto, Bernard's wife, handled all of his correspondence. The thought of the gifted, sage, and canny Avis handling her husband's fan mail a la Vera Nabokov who, I read once, also escorted her husband around when it rained, to save him having to clutter his mind with learning to open an umbrella, is another rant for another time.* In any case, Avis answered Julia's letter, and the two became devoted pen pals, then best friends, confidantes, and colleagues. Julia would refer to her, alternately, as her "wet nurse" and her "mentor."

Their letters are astonishing, a primer both on what it means to be a good friend and why people loved Julia the way they did. When DeVoto, as Avis referred to him, won the National

---

* DeVoto had been Avis's English professor at Northwestern; how could the balance of the marriage been any different?

Book Award, Julia leaned hard into her congratulations, raving for a solid sincere paragraph about his achievement. She always inquired about Avis's work, health, and sons,* and they jointly railed against Republicans, McCarthyism, books they'd read and loved and hated, even the findings in the Kinsey Reports on human sexual behavior.† Their letters were tender and conscientious. Once Julia apologized for failing to send more biographical details about Simca and Louisette and promised them next time, along with "a nice photo of a cold decorated fish."

Mostly, they rhapsodized about cooking, and about Julia's big book project. Reading through these long, euphoric letters to Avis, you'd be forgiven for wondering whether Julia was on something other than a beautiful Bordeaux 1929. She enthused over the pure beauty of white beans, the eye-watering bite of some garlic sausages, the heavenly ham hocks, tiny French strawberries, which she called dreamberries. I'm perfectly willing to accept that I don't possess the foodie gene that inspires me to speak in tongues when in the presence of the year's first crop of string beans, but neither did Julia. In her rather heavily documented life, there are few foodgasms before she met Paul: She rhapsodized dutifully about her mother's codfish balls and Welsh rarebit and waxes nostalgic about tooting down to Tijuana with her family to try something called a Caesar salad, but otherwise she seemed to be a born food-as-fuel gal.

---

* Avis had two, one of whom was "troubled," and likely suffered from what we now call Asperger's syndrome.

† As we know, Julia was wildly interested in the subject.

What changed?

My theory, extrapolated from years of watching Dr. Huang of *Law & Order SVU: Special Victims Unit* explain why people (usually deranged criminals) behave in ways the rest of us find inexplicable, is that every time Julia perfected a dish, she was revisiting the rapture of her life's grandest transitional moment, the Day of the Sole Meunière in Rouen. It was her own private Eucharist, celebrating love, the senses, the joy of sex and intimacy, and the transformation of a lost girl, now found.

Even though she came, eventually, to stand for celebrating the glory of our imperfect, overseared pork chops, and potato pancakes we accidentally dropped on the floor, she knew that occasionally a dish could be perfect, and a life could be perfect, for just that moment. Like every superhero, Julia had that origin story, and in making *Mastering* she was given an opportunity to relive it. She was both enjoying and documenting in the recipes her own self-discovery, that which, finally, in middle age gave her life its meaning.

During those years in which she labored over *Mastering the Art of French Cooking,* she lived in a state of more or less permanent jubilation, spending her days in "flow," that hippie-sounding term that describes a feeling of complete absorption in the task at hand.*

Happiness studies are all the rage now, even though all the ancient philosophers, including Unknown and Anonymous,

---

* Not to be confused with "going with the flow," it was first defined in 1975 by psychologist Mihaly Csikszentmihalyi, who would probably be more famous had he changed his name to something like Michael Hale. If you're reading this, Mr Csiksz . . . whatever, it's not too late.

insist that happiness is a by-product of something else, like being busy (Mark Twain), limiting our desires (John Stuart Mill), or letting go (The Buddha). My idea of happiness is doing something with your life that echoes a time when you were 100 percent sure you were happy.*

A friend of mine had a son who loved playing "office" when he was small, and he has grown up to be the happiest† contracts attorney I know. Likewise, the world is full of people who opted for business school or marketing careers either because they weren't lucky enough to find something that put them in a swoon, or they needed a career, and one seemed as good as any other. Almost always they find out, too late, that one is not as good as any other.

Julia worked hard and worked happy for a good half century. How did she do it?

Throw yourself into it, even when no one cares but you.
Mayonnaise is relatively easy to make. Julia mastered it early. Often, when the cooking wasn't going well and she was pulling

---

* The exception to my theory is becoming a rock star. All kids want to be rock stars, because they assume being on stage will make them as happy as they are belting out a song in their room into the end of their hairbrush; this happiness can never be duplicated.

† Which is to say, the only happy one.

out her hair, ruining pound after pound of *escalope de veau*,* she would whip up a pint or two to boost her confidence. Combine an egg yolk with half a cup of oil and add a few tablespoons of vinegar or lemon juice. Voilà, mayonnaise.

Then one day the yolk would not accept the oil or the oil would not mingle with the egg, or something was going on. Julia did exactly what she always did, but she wound up with something closer to mucus than mayonnaise. She was flummoxed. Why did her recipe, which had never failed her, suddenly fail her? Learning to cook had awakened Julia's inner voluptuary, but this was something else. Apparently, it was not enough to be able to make something, document how you got there, and call it a recipe; you also had to know why the food did what it did, so that if something changed (What changed? Hadn't she made mayonnaise the way she always made mayonnaise?) you could modify your technique.

Thus Julia's inner scientist was born. Cooking was worthy of being her life's passion because it was the only thing, aside from her love of Paul, that kept revealing new parts of herself.

How could Julia have known she had an inner, exacting chemist? This now nearly middle-aged woman who had no apparent aptitude for science was now consumed with how cooking *worked*. She was obsessed with her failed mayonnaise.

---

* Veal scallops, which "make a perfect main course for a chic little luncheon." She struggled mightily with browning them. Many books advised browning "slowly," but how slow was slow? Too slow and the meat refused to brown, too quickly and the butter threatened to burn.

Was it the temperature of the egg yolk? The temperature of the bowl? The temperature in the kitchen? Would mixing it with a fork guarantee perfection?* Did it make a difference whether you added the oil all at once? Fast or slow? Slow at first, then faster? Drop by drop?

She was now no simple Foreign Service wife dutifully throwing together a meal for her hardworking husband. This was something else, a woman on a mission to find the answer to something meaningful only to her. She spent days making nothing but mayonnaise. She made so much mayonnaise, even Paul, who ate and relished everything she cooked, said *No more,* and she was forced to dump gallons of it down the commode. Finally, triumphant, she recorded her discovery,† and she mailed it to all her friends and family. Let's pause to remember the effort this took in 1950: the typing, the procuring of the proper postage stamps, the mailing, the waiting for a response. The result: complete silence.

Julia became obsessed over the molecular structure of potatoes and wrote to the U.S. Department of Agriculture to see if they might offer any insight.‡ She educated herself on the best part of the cow's stomach to use for tripe, and if anyone cared, which part of an egg yolk is the core. Once, she threw a dinner

----

* No, it absolutely must be a wire whisk.

† Her mayonnaise recipe had stopped working because summer had turned to fall and yolk, oil, and bowl were all too cold. Slightly warming the bowl before beginning fixed everything.

‡ They sent her two pamphlets. She swooned.

party and served sea bass with a beurre blanc sauce that wouldn't "blanc." *Why?* She was astounded, believing she had her beurre blanc down cold. The next morning she made six more batches to make sure she got it right. She did all this because it interested her to know, not because it was necessary for writing the cookbook, although it wound up being absolutely necessary because it lent *Mastering* the authority it enjoys to this day.

I am sobered when I think of how much of Julia's cooking life was spent satisfying her own curiosity. For me, cooking remains confusing, all wrapped up in housewifery, in being the body attached to the arm attached to the hand that holds the plate of steaming food, in being the woman, in her place, in the kitchen. Home cooks cook because someone is hungry or there is going to be a celebration that demands food. A recent episode of *Downton Abbey,* the British upstairs/downstairs soap opera, touched on the dilemma when Mrs. Patmore, the head cook of the Abbey, feared and obeyed by all the young kitchen maids beneath her, is courted by a local produce purveyor. This would have been the last chance at romance for Mrs. Patmore, but she turns him down, realizing he only wanted her for her cooking, and that she would rather oversee the tremendous daily work of making the meals for the Crawleys of Downton Abbey than be at the endless beck and call of a husband who demanded his pudding made just so.

But cooking aside, how often do you—do any of us—work that hard at something simply to find the answers to questions no one else is asking but us? Whatever modern strides have been made in feminism, women, it seems to me, are as tied to results, by which I mean pleasing others, as we ever were. The woman I consider to be my most successful friend—lucratively self-employed with a sweet and handsome husband, lovely kids—swears by her To Do List. She loves her To Do List. She has blogged hilariously and with great affection about her To Do List. I asked to see it and was surprised, given her success, that not one thing on it was something she did purely out of her own curiosity. When I asked her about this she laughed and said, "Who has time for curiosity for curiosity's sake?" But what made her happy? Her family, of course. Her lucrative career, of course. But what else? "Getting to the end of the day," she said, "and knowing I've finished my To Do List."

Do not cater to the flimsies.
Julia was a stickler for proper cooking technique but was free and easy when it came to language. When she couldn't find what she considered to be the proper word or phrase, she made up her own. Some of her favorites, in no particular order:

Person Traitoria: A traitor, specifically herself, in relation to her right-of-Joe-McCarthy father.

Dogmatic Meatball: a blowhard, usually French, who believed his way was the only way, and who patronized her because she had two strikes against her, being both female and American.

Upper Middle Brow: Her people ("distressing examples of conspicuous waste of good human material"). Next to being sloppy and taking shortcuts, the biggest insult in Julia's arsenal.

Upper Bohemians: Her new tribe. Paul and Avis belonged to this class. They read books.

A&P Garboozova: All the god-awful grocery store items passing for food in America: frozen TV dinners, margarine, Cheez Whiz.

Bilious: Any kind of digestive ailment (bloating, nausea, the feeling that the blood in your veins is being replaced by cream) that results from overeating too many test recipes.

Phoo: Short for phooey.

Fluffies: People into "gourmet" cooking. She thought the word *gourmet* was pretentious, as were the fluffies.

Flimsies: People who didn't take cooking seriously, who must never be catered to.

"Flimsies" is such a ridiculous word, but Julia was serious. She, who'd never been taken seriously before, was serious on every front on which she could be: serious about not allowing anyone to condescend to her because she was a mere housewife; serious about behaving like a professional, even as she was still learning; serious about refusing to dumb down her recipes to make them seem less daunting to her readership;* and perhaps most important, serious about her procedures, which were the actions that spoke louder than her words.

She tested and retested every recipe in Simca and Louisette's book and rewrote every one. She had to find out everything for herself, had to see it with her own eyes. If Simca, Louisette, or Avis, or one of the trusted friends back in the States who were trying out her recipes as she was completing them came up with a different result, she would try the recipe again, to see if she could duplicate it.

When the time came to tackle cassoulet, the iconic comfort food casserole from the south of France—pork sausage, goose, and white haricot beans cooked for days in a heavy earthenware pot—Julia rounded up twenty-eight recipes, all from chefs who claimed, in Dogmatic Meatball–style, that their recipe was the *correct* recipe.

Reader, she made them all.

She was determined to Americanize dishes that most people could go to their grave without knowing how to make. Fish quenelles is one. The first clue is that there is no English translation. A quenelle is a quenelle is a quenelle. The second is the phrase "force the fish through the strainer." All that comes to mind is a scene from *Alien Resurrection,* where the massive, gleaming half-human/half-alien is sucked out of a golf ball–size

---

* Supposing there was one: She was counting on the American housewife/chauffeur not to be as flimsy as she appeared.

air hole and into deep space, viscera first. Still, Julia thought we should all know about them.*

Most of *Mastering* was written via mail.† In 1953, not long after Julia began working in earnest, Paul was posted to Marseille, which they loved (still France) and then to Plattsdorf, Germany (not so much). They spent some time back in Washington, D.C, then went on to Oslo, Norway. There was no question that Julia would accompany him. Where Paul went, Julia went. They were Pulia. Julia packed up her *batterie de cuisine* (totaling seventy-two pots, pans, graters, extractors, squeezers, and whisks) and unpacked it again in some too-small kitchen with too-low counters in another city, so that she could continue working on the book.

Still, it didn't matter where she was; her work ethic was something not seen often among people in this century. In their little government-issue apartment in Plattsdorf, which Julia more or less despised, she nevertheless set herself the task of learning German. After cooking most of the day, she would finish up writing recipes around 7:00 p.m. and cook dinner to be served at 8:00 p.m. Then she and Paul would "fritter" away an hour (during which she would relax by writing detailed, hilarious ten-page letters to Avis), after which she would study German for a few hours.

---

* Guess what? They don't have to be made of strained fish. The name also refers to the soft, footballish shape. There can be ice-cream and mashed potato quenelles, too.

† Simca's letters were written in French. Think of it. Julia had spoken fluent French for about six minutes, and here came the communications from her collaborator, written in that spiky European hand.

Though she often wanted to bash Simca over the head for some *La Super-Française* outburst, she was rarely unhappy.

It's not a new observation: Throwing ourselves into hard work can be deeply gratifying, and mastering a skill is a satisfaction in and of itself, but the reality of this has largely fallen out of favor. In our modern times, people generally feel that the key to happiness involves doing the least amount of work for the most glory, believing that happiness is to be found in outward appreciation and approval, not inner dedication. That this never really makes anyone happy—witness the miserable reality stars, the depressed lottery winners—fails to deter us; we somehow remain convinced that the smart money is on figuring out a way to grab the gold ring with the least amount of effort.

Is there something you're dying to attempt, but you manage to talk yourself out of it because it seems like too much work, or will take too much time and discipline? This is your inner flimsy talking. Pat her on the head, but don't cater to her. You'll be happier for it.

Do everything humanly possible to avoid housework.
Part of the immense gastro-cultural divide between a hallowed Michelin star–studded French chef and the Servantless American Cook was that the chef devoted every waking hour to his art, and of course had someone at home to cook for him and care for him, while the SAC, as well as her family, which she was there

to serve, considered cooking to be part of her many chores. You know, the ones that are never done, per the old saying.

Over the years, so much snark has been directed at those Franco-American Spaghetti, frozen French cut string bean–serving housewives, who really can't be blamed for wanting to make their lives a little easier. We are now enlightened, and know about using the best fresh produce, using the caramelized nubs of meat left in the pan to make a sauce, the miracle of cooking something down to intensify the flavor, and all the basics instilled in our grandmothers and mothers by Julia, Craig Claiborne, James Beard, and all the other kitchen heroes who rescued America from Mrs. Paul's Frozen Fish Sticks and Tang. But the end of a long day is still the end of a long day—ask any Busy Stay-at-Home Mom.* And often the impulse to order a pizza is overwhelming, especially since it's all your kids will eat anyway.

That said, if you want to devote any time to cooking seriously, or doing anything seriously for that matter, something has got to go, and that something is housework. If hiring someone to come in every other week means giving up your daily latte or buying shoes at PayLess, do it. You are giving someone else gainful employment, escaping the admonition of V. I. Lenin, who railed that "petty housework crushes, strangles, stultifies and degrades" women, and being like Julia, who did as little as possible.

---

* The modern iteration of the Average American Housewife. In the same way every American housewife was once "average," every stay-at-home mom is now "busy."

RULE <u>No.</u> 7:

SOLVE THE PROBLEM IN FRONT OF YOU

⚜

If you get nervous, just sit back and think about it, and then plunge in and do it again.

APRIL IN PARIS, IT TURNS OUT, IS A LOT LIKE APRIL IN PORTLAND. The drear and rain don't seem like weather, changeable and possibly exciting, but like an occupy movement, here to stay. Kathy and I took the Metro to the Bastille and walked through Place des Vosges to the Marais, having conceived a need to stroll through one of our favorite neighborhoods on the way to the famed E. Dehillerin, about a mile away on the rue Coquillière, where Julia spent a lot of her inheritance outfitting her world-class *batterie de cuisine*. Despite the slanting rain, we had umbrellas—and I had brought along a brown GORE-TEX jacket (with hood) that was so utilitarian it caused several shopkeepers and waiters to address me in German—and we saw no reason to change our itinerary. Especially since you can't eat as we had been eating and still expect to have anything resembling a waist.

The great unspoken dilemma of cooking as Julia would wish us to is that, arteriosclerosis aside, if you sit quietly you can feel your muffin top growing. Until the very end of her life, when she looks not fat, but rectangular, like a refrigerator box, Julia was slim-waisted as an athlete. Even on *The French Chef,* in her early fifties, with her cotton blouse around her midriff, her apron strings are tied neatly across her flat belly.*

I have many slender friends who identify as foodies and who spend an inordinate amount of time cooking, but you also never see them eating anything. One acquaintance, who resembles a Modigliani model, never visits anyone without bringing a homemade cheesecake or batch of lemon bars. Another is famed for her stupendous Italian sausage three-cheese lasagna, made with whole-fat ricotta; the last time she served it, she stuck to the dark leafy salad with a whisper of vinaigrette. I'm mystified by this behavior, and suspect it may be cuisinerexia, where the satisfaction is to be found in working your ass off making terrific food and then denying yourself the pleasure of eating it, but at least it makes sense why these women are thin.

But Julia cooked all day, tasting everything, and also ate breakfast, tucked into a nice lunch, and cooked dinner for her husband, as well as the cavalcade of visiting dignitaries, cultural attachés, and diplomats he was obligated to entertain. People who like to eat are the best people, and Julia was one of the best people of all, and Kathy and I wanted to be part of that tribe,

---

* Lest we forget, the camera puts on ten pounds.

and so we cooked and tasted and ate, and the pounds threatened
to pile on like a passel of drunken brothers-in-law at the annual
Thanksgiving family football game.

How did Julia manage it? When posed with that question,
Julia advocated moderation in all things, even moderation, and
we believed her. How did we manage to overlook the fact that
she was six foot three—bigger than most men—and probably
had the metabolism to match, bringing to mind my six foot two
inches father who, the moment he accrued an inch of spare tire,
gave up the bowl of Dried Planter's Peanuts that accompanied
his nightly martini for a week or so and off it came.

At any rate, Kathy and I are both a mere five foot eight, and
to counteract the effects of all the round, yellow, buttery things
we were cooking and devouring—various omelets, the Gateau
de Crêpes à la Florentine*—we vowed that during the day, if we
weren't cooking, we would be walking.

The Marais was crowded, with tourists and Parisians and
a gang of Orthodox men and boys in blue suits and big hats
and with long Pe'ot on their way to temple. Not blocks from
the shop, we passed a girl sobbing on the sidewalk, surrounded
by two women who stood very close to her. They were all the
same height, all with the same dark hair and dark, chic French
clothes, all very upright. It's unusual to see a Parisian sobbing on
the street; we walked on and at the intersection saw lying on the

---

*A giant stack of crêpes—we used twenty-four—between which are slathered alternating layers
of a spinach/Mornay sauce filling and a mushroom/cream cheese filling, topped with a healthy
grating of Parmigiano-Reggiano cheese and dotted with butter. We ovenless home cooks
melted the cheese in the microwave.

ground a tall, thin young man who looked as if he had keeled over and hit his head on the curb. An emergency vehicle was there, and two policemen were there, both sort of leaning over and peeking at the side of his face. No one touched him. Was he hit by a car? An aneurysm, maybe? He looked like a tree felled in the forest, and he was clearly dead.

It was Saturday, and E. Dehillerin was packed with shoppers and oglers and their dripping umbrellas. The business is 193 years old, the building much older. Chefs bring their copper pots here to be retinned. The raw-beamed ceilings soar, the wooden floorboards groan and creak, and the aisles are narrow enough to make a claustrophobe break out in a sweat. There's a mildew-smelling house-parts place in Portland that sells doorknobs and light fixtures foraged from condemned houses and Dehillerin smells the same, and shares the same spirit of We Are above Displaying Any of These Treasures to Their Best Advantage.

It was all there: the stuff Julia geeked out over, everything you would ever need to cook anything, and a lot of things whose uses you wouldn't understand even after someone explained them to you. The pots, sauté pans, skillets, roasting pans, and sauciers. The aspic molds and soufflé dishes. The enameled cast-iron Dutch ovens and ceramic baking dishes. The colanders, couscoussiers, and crêpe pans. The poultry scissors and brass-plated duck press. An entire aisle of pitted wooden shelves displaying rows of what appear to be tin loaf pans filled with every kind of knife on earth. A wall of whisks, separated according to size—pinky finger to baseball bat—in individual wooden cubbies.

A cream-colored pegboard, not unlike the one Paul made for Julia, rose to the ceiling; dozens of the famous Dehillerin tin-lined copper pots hung in haphazard lines. I pulled down a saucepan, appreciated its heft. There was no price tag on it, but I know from my online research that this size runs about sixty-five euros ($85).

As it happened, I had just finished reading (and loving) *My Kitchen Wars,* Betty Fussell's great caustic memoir of marriage and cooking. Fussell, a cookbook author, food historian, and, by her own admission, angry, overeducated housewife, is only a year younger than my mother would have been, and *Mastering the Art of French Cooking* changed her life, just as it did my mother's

She raved about how Julia gave her, and all of her friends, permission to treat cooking—"the one activity, besides tennis, in which housewives were encouraged to excel"—as an art. She wrote about how Julia insisted that the servantless American cook have proper, professional tools, sending Betty and her friends dashing in their suburban station wagons into Manhattan from the New Jersey suburbs to buy tin-lined copper pots, with the requisite minimum one-eighth-inch-thick bottoms. "This was no undertaking for the poor," wrote Betty Fussell.

Standing in Dehillerin, holding the copper saucepan, I remember reading that section and thinking, *Huh, really? We weren't rich,* and then coming to a sentence farther down on the page: "Out went the Revere Ware at the first Hospital Charity Sale."

Not at our house it didn't, I thought. Even though we had a dishwasher, every night I washed our Revere Ware by hand, "to keep it nice." Nice being maintaining the cheap copper wash on the stainless-steel bottom. My mother watched *The French Chef* in the den of our Southern California tract house in Whittier, with a steno pad on her knee. In the cupboard of her orange and yellow kitchen, gold-veined mirror tiles installed over the sink to "open up the room," her copy of *Mastering* had folded-back corners and wine-stained pages, just as did the copies of the more educated, much more sophisticated Fussell.

The allure of Julia Child, my mother once said to me, was that she believed in doing things right. My mother cooked like a mad fool with her Revere Ware and "oven-safe" Pyrex baking dishes, and even though I longed only for Taco Night, I knew my mother's food, her coq au vin and veal scallops, her beef bourguignon and Dover sole sautéed in some damn thing, was good. I imagine it's a tribute to both Julia and my mother that she managed it with such crappy, low-brow cookware.

I put the saucepan back on the pegboard, although for a minute I thought about putting it on my head, as I used to my mother's Revere Ware, when I was in a mood. I remembered that my own daughter used to wear my Revere Ware on her head as well. Was it genetic? Or a silent, subconscious reminder from little daughters to dutiful mothers throughout the ages: Remember the silly fun to be had with these pots and pans?

There's no checkout counter to speak of at Dehillerin. There are frazzled Frenchmen with rolled cuffs and stubby pencils behind their ears who figure out how much you owe on a scrap of paper and then send you with your items and the bill to a desk, over which hangs a faded black-and-white still of Julia as The French Chef, behind not one, but two protective plastic covers.

THE ROAD TO SUCCESS AND THE ROAD TO FAILURE ARE ALMOST EXACTLY THE SAME*

At the end of 1956, Paul was summoned home by the State Department for home leave, and he and Julia resettled in the house they'd purchased just after they were married on the outskirts of Georgetown, in Washington, D.C. Julia used some of her inheritance money to renovate the kitchen: new gas range, dishwasher, and a "pig" (an in-sink garbage disposal), readying herself for the final push in completing what she and Simca had come to call, simply, The Book. Simca came from France,† and they worked fourteen-hour days, completing the final poultry recipes and retesting some of the first sauce recipes they'd concocted five years earlier. They enjoyed that special hell reserved for people who've spent so long on a project that the sheer effort of creating it has forced them to evolve into such different people

---

* Colin R. Davis, a British conductor known mostly for his repertoire of Mozart, Berlioz, and Stravinsky, whose uplifting bons mots show up on the Internet a lot, usually accompanied by a picture of a beautiful sunrise or a determined-looking sparrow.

† Or at least I think she did. Julia mentioned Simca's visit in a letter to Avis, but in her new introduction written for the fortieth-anniversary edition, she says that Simca didn't come to the States until their book tour in 1961. *Ça ne fait rien.*

from the ones who'd launched into it years earlier; all the early work, once thought to be excellent, is seen for what it is: the work of someone just starting out.

At the same time, prompted by both Avis and the people at Houghton Mifflin, Julia tried to place some of their recipes with *Good Housekeeping, Ladies' Home Journal,* and other women's magazines. Julia gave it a shot, but she disparaged the "ladies magaziney" approach to a lot of cooking—like using a paper bag to dredge a piece of poultry in flour instead of just using your hands—and she was disappointed when she found no takers. Even her simplest recipes were deemed too difficult. Editors replied saying that not only were Julia's highly detailed, complex instructions a waste of time but also in some cases they were, frankly, a little demented.

One of her original motivations in writing the book was to clarify and unpack confusing instructions that had become accepted as part of cookbook vernacular. "Brown the chicken" means what, exactly? "Sauté the mushrooms": Is that like browning the mushrooms in the same way you brown the chicken? Do you cover the pan? Do you stir them or bounce them around, or what? "Add the cream and wine": Which one goes first or does it matter? Do you stir them in?

In her recipes, "detailed" and "complicated" as they were, Julia was attempting to banish forever the vague language that tripped up home cooks, giving them a way to re-create the same perfect dish now and forever more. Before Julia, recipes were not unlike the one for gingerbread that M.F.K. Fisher rhapsodizes about in *Serve It Forth*. After the "old black honey, the older and blacker the better" is heated and combined with flour, the cook is instructed to put the resulting paste in a cold place for as long as she can.[*] When she can stand it no longer, she retrieves the bowl, adds the rest of the ingredients, and then is instructed to beat it "for a painfully long time."

That said, as right as Julia would turn out to be, she wasn't always as in touch with her audience as she imagined herself to be. While magazine and book editors tended to view housewives as being only a few IQ points smarter than a well-trained Labrador retriever, and with much less daring,[†] Julia sometimes overestimated their dedication and underestimated their degree of squeamishness.[‡] In her effort to help home cooks with their pressed duck, she suggested that since it was unlikely they would be able to find a duck that had been suffocated rather than shot—there is too much blood loss when they are shot; duck blood is necessary for enriching the taste of the sauce—"go ahead as so many French restaurants do now, and add fresh pig's blood mixed with wine to the duck press." A terrific suggestion, had her goal been to create a nation of vegetarians.

----

[*] In Dijon, famous for their *pain d'épices*, and where this particular recipe is said to have originated, the chilling time could be from several months to several years.

[†] They seemed one and all concerned that the housewife would find a monster, multipaged recipe "frightening."

[‡] Julia was only slightly less squeamish than Sweeney Todd.

The first deadline for The Book was February 24, 1958. The official title was *French Cooking for the American Kitchen,* and it was nearly eight hundred pages long.

The story has been told many times, how Julia and Simca delivered an unwieldy behemoth, not the smart French cookbook geared for the American housewife/chauffeur that Houghton Mifflin had contracted for, but a mad, not to say obsessive, compilation of every sauce and poultry recipe in the known French culinary universe. Still to be addressed were eggs, vegetables, fish, meat, and desserts. In a letter to Avis, Julia wrote, "We intend to take an attack position. That this is the type of series of books we plan to do, and that Volume II will be ready well within a year of the publication of Vol. I; and that Volume III will be ready within about six months of Volume II. This is going to mean hard and constant application but we feel it must be done . . ."

Houghton Mifflin did not feel the same, and it was a good thing, too. Eight hundred pages of sauces and poultry? As Dorothy de Santillana pointed out in her respectful rejection letter, length aside, the two don't have anything in common, aside from the fact that Julia and Simca happened to focus on those sections first. Oh, I know. The romance of this kind of saga demands that the suits get a bad rap for thinking only of the bottom line, for quashing Julia's creative integrity and genius, but the meanies and the pencil pushers aren't always wrong. Houghton Mifflin saved Julia from herself and helped her to refocus. In case there's any doubt, after Julia became the most famous cook in America, with a spate of best-selling cookbooks and a hit TV show, with Emmys, honorary doctorate degrees, and a running spot on *Good Morning America,* did she call Judith Jones on her private line at Knopf and say, "We must publish an eight-hundred-page book on sauces and poultry?" No, she did not.

Her letter acknowledging the rejection letter was determinedly upbeat, her attack position abandoned. She acknowledged that what she and Simca had slaved away on was not what they'd been contracted to do, and that they were prepared to write a "short and snappy book directed to the somewhat sophisticated housewife/chauffeur" of about three hundred pages that would include "unusual vegetable dishes including the pepping up of canned and frozen vegetables" and, hopefully, even "insert a note of gaiety and a certain quiet chic."

Julia was frustrated and heart-bruised. Avis, who never lost the faith, consoled her with the truth that nothing we learn ever goes to waste, and that someday her work would pay off.

It could not be said of Julia that she was no quitter. She'd quit quite a few things in her time. At Smith she quit the basketball team when it was obvious she wasn't the star her mother had been. She quit the Packard Commercial School after a mere month,* quit her good job at W. & J. Sloane and New York City entirely after she'd been jilted by Tom, her literature major boyfriend. Julia's passion and sense of theatrics cut both ways; she could throw herself out of something as easily as she could throw herself into it.

---

*And, who can blame her?

There was no reason why she shouldn't have quit The Book, too. Why persist? The project had occupied her time, given her a sense of purpose, and enriched her life beyond measure, while Paul was overworking at his various embassies. Creating The Book had given her a *métier* and a *raison d'être,* words that find feeble translation in English. Also, unlike writing an eight-hundred-page novel that no one wants, the recipes you've created for a cookbook are useful. You still have to eat. It's the nature of cookery-bookery that several times a day you can still practice the thing that inspired you to want to write a cookbook in the first place. Indeed, for people who have a tortured ambivalence about cooking, the exact same thing plunges us into Sisyphean despair, that not ninety minutes after we've cleaned up after one meal it's time to start preparing the next one. But this is cause for great joy for a devoted foodie like Julia. She and Paul would still need to eat, and she could still cook up a storm, dirtying every copper pot in the place. That would never change.

It couldn't have helped her frame of mind to witness first-hand the state of American cuisine. She and Paul had been abroad for many years, and they had only heard about the invasion of entire frozen meals that were served in the compartmentalized tin tray in which they were heated and then consumed on trays in front of the television. Julia and Paul didn't own a television, nor had they ever watched it. Craig Claiborne, the then-new food editor and restaurant critic for the *New York Times,* bemoaned the state of cooking in America.

At any rate, life was moving on. Paul had just accepted a posting in Norway, at the Cultural Affairs Office in Oslo. Publicly she was grateful for the posting—Paul needed to work, and this was a promotion—but Julia sobbed in private at the thought of packing up her *batterie de cuisine* and leaving her new gas range, the dishwasher, and pig in the sink for another tiny kitchen in another foreign country that was not France.

The obvious lesson in all this, knowing how it all turned out, is that when faced with a setback of this magnitude, there is nothing for it but to pick yourself up, dust yourself off, and soldier on with renewed determination to succeed! If only it were that easy. Julia was in a funk. How did she manage to persevere, turning a stupendous failure into a groundbreaking success?

Keep trying, keep failing.
Paul and Julia sailed for Europe on the SS *United States,* stopping in France for a few days to indulge in a bilious-inducing tour of their favorite restaurants and see old, beloved friends. Julia's first friend in Paris, Hélène Baltrusaitis, had just organized a special exhibit at the US Information Agency (USIA), Paul's old haunt: "The Twenties: American Writers in Paris and Their Friends." Julia and Paul missed the exhibit by a few days, but not the chance to make the acquaintance of Sylvia Beach, owner of Shakespeare and Company and publisher of *Ulysses.* If anything could coax the famously reclusive playwright Samuel

Beckett from his hidey-hole on the rue des Favorites, it would be a celebration of his beloved James Joyce.

Until the end of her long life, Julia was never afraid to seek the advice of experts.

In all the Western world, no one was a bigger expert on failure than Beckett. If Julia was happiest in the kitchen, the author of *Waiting for Godot* was happiest in the pit of despair. Who better, then, to advise her on how to go on when you simply couldn't go on?

They met for dinner at La Closerie des Lilas on Boulevard du Montparnasse and sat on the lamp-lit terrace. Since it was spring, chances are it was depressing and gray, just the kind of weather Beckett preferred. Inside, the same piano player who entertained Hemingway, Picasso, Apollinaire, and all the rest, played his old standards. The two feasted on escargots with garlic and parsley butter, duck foie gras terrine, steak tartare, and white asparagus. They enjoyed one of those beautiful, perfectly matured Bordeaux that made Julia swoon.

Beckett, who resembled a bird-of-prey, with his large, bony nose and thick, cowlicky, stand-up gray hair, was known to be a man of few words. But Julia wielded her polecat-charming genius and had him waxing philosophical before the end of the first course. He nodded sagely—also something at which he was an expert—as he listened to her tale of cookery-bookery woe, then reminded her that as long as you take even one step forward you haven't failed.

Success was complicated, he said, but failure is easy. All you had to do was keep going, one step at a time. All you had to do was solve the problem in front of you.

"Try again. Fail again. Fail better," he said, over the cheese course.

Of course, this meal is a figment of my butter-addled imagination. This meal never happened, or not that any of the Julia scholars know of, but given how Julia proceeded, it might have. She spent the last two days in Paris working with Simca, who was recovering from an attack of gout, on a failed recipe for *jambon en croûte*, determined to give Houghton Mifflin a cookbook they would be proud to publish.

Try again. Fail again. Fail better.
Given Julia's dedication to doing things right, her passion for teaching, and her aversion to shortcuts, she was never going to be able to produce the "short and snappy" three-hundred pages she promised Dorothy de Santillana. Even if she could do it, there's every chance that Avis, who was not only her best friend, confidant, and mentor, but also an important publishing-world contact, would not have let her.

Avis was that outlier, the most excellent housewife-chauffeur, and Julia's perfect reader. Without Avis, there could have been no Julia Child, The French Chef. Houghton Mifflin was DeVoto's publisher, and it was Avis who hooked Les Trois Gourmandes up with Dorothy Santillana, but her greatest gift was guiding Julia so that her zeal didn't get in the way of her message.

Julia loved French cuisine only a smidge less than she loved Paul: the discipline it required and the respect it demanded, but she was also, at heart, a populist. She wanted the people most disparaged by the world of gastronomy—American housewives—to have a shot at making something great to eat. She was on a mission to demystify French cuisine. She was Toto, pulling away the curtain to reveal the Great Oz.

Despite her dedication to process, about taking the proper amount of time and never heeding the siren call of shortcuts, Julia was never a food snob. Once, when she and Paul were living in Germany, they made a trip back to the States, and she claimed the only good thing she ate was a foot-long hot dog with sauerkraut. When they moved back to the States, for good, settling not far from where Avis lived in Cambridge, Massachusetts, Julia went on record as saying the only thing wrong with McDonald's was that they didn't serve red wine.

In editing the original book-length chapter of sauces and poultry, Julia struggled to simplify, while still being thorough. She'd gotten the message, finally, that for someone who wasn't naturally and perpetually high on life, love, cooking, and Paris, her recipes could be a lot of work, especially since her potential readers suffered a dilemma completely foreign to French women: having to bust ass in the kitchen while being expected, at the same time, to float among their guests, the serene hostess. Even when she and Paul remodeled their kitchen in Georgetown, she refused to entertain the notion of installing a professional stove, because she knew her housewife audience would never own such a thing. To that end, she tried to structure her recipes so that some steps could be done in advance.

Avis was a genius at helping Julia strike the right balance. Reading the first draft Avis made a note, "I have a strong impression that very few American butchers these days know how to pull tendons." Yet she also encouraged her not to dumb down the book: "Use finesse as often as you like—once you have explained what it means once or twice."

Julia and Simca put their heads together and spent another year culling, rewriting, and simplifying. Sauces and poultry needed only to be edited; sections on fish, meat, vegetables, entree and luncheon dishes, cold buffet, and desserts and cakes were brand new. They argued, sometimes bitterly. Simca, in her *La Super-Française*-mode, shrieked at the idea of using a canned or frozen vegetable in even one recipe.

Most of the work was done while Julia was in Oslo, where she was reminded of her mission every so often. Once, at a luncheon for embassy wives, they served for the main course a "salad" made of pink mayonnaise, frozen strawberries, peaches, dates, and bananas with whipped cream—a lone piece of iceberg lettuce peeped out from underneath—followed by a piece of banana cake from a mix, with thick lard frosting. Julia snorted and declared it a "triumph of Norwegian/American *McCallism*," after the magazine that rejected her recipes.

When she wasn't involved in her cookery-bookery or teaching one of her cooking classes (she ran two, with eight students each), she and Paul hiked and skied. She found Norway and the Norwegians to be "nifty." She devoted herself to learning Norwegian, and by the time she left she could read it and could understand half of any given theater performance. She dutifully practiced with her cleaning lady and the shopkeepers but despaired a little because her Norwegian friends all spoke English.

Finally, in September 1959, the new version of the cookbook was ready. Julia's promise that it would be a short, snappy three hundred pages was made by a distraught, exhausted author desperate to fulfill her contract and salvage something from her years of long hard work. It was never going to happen. In preparation for submitting the new, slimmer seven-hundred-and-fifty-page manuscript, Julia wrote a letter explaining: "Good French food cannot be produced by zombie cooks," she said, "one must be willing to sweat over it."

It took only two months for Houghton Mifflin to reject it again.

She then sent the following letter:

Dearest Simca and Avis,
Black news on the cookbook front . . . The answer is NO,
Neg, Non, Nein . . . too expensive to print, no prospects of a

mass audience . . . We must accept the fact that this may well be a book unacceptable to any publisher, as it requires work on the part of the reader . . .

Julia was beginning to loathe the housewife-chauffeur, the chauffeur–den mother, whatever they wanted to call this apparently lazy, easily intimidated, yet powerful, creature to whom commerce was in thrall. She licked her wounds by throwing herself into learning about French pastry, heretofore her weak spot.

But Avis, who had worked as a book scout at Alfred A. Knopf, had already sent it to a senior editor named Bill Koshland, who passed it on to a junior editor named Judith Jones. Both of them were the rare book people who loved to cook. Persevering is often not simply a matter of working hard and refusing to quit; often, by trying again, failing again, and failing better, we inadvertently place ourselves in the way of luck. Yet another reason to keep on keeping on.

Rule No. 8:

Cooking Means Never Saying You're Sorry

❧

The only real stumbling block is fear of failure.

In January 1961, John F. Kennedy was inaugurated. He was only forty-three, the youngest president in history. He created the Peace Corps, cut diplomatic ties with Cuba, recovered from the embarrassment of the Bay of Pigs fiasco, and sent nine hundred political advisors to Saigon, officially kicking off the Vietnam War. His elegant wife, Jackie, had a French maiden name and employed a French chef in the White House kitchen.

"The Twist" was one of the year's most popular dance tunes, and Bob Dylan made his debut in Greenwich Village. Barack Obama was born in Honolulu. In October, *Breakfast at Tiffany's* was in theaters, *The Dick Van Dyke Show* premiered on TV, and *Mastering the Art of French Cooking: The Only Cookbook That Explains How to Create Authentic French Dishes in*

*American Kitchens with American Food** was published to considerable fanfare.

"Probably the most comprehensive, laudable, and monumental work on [French cuisine] was published this week, and it will probably remain as the definitive work for non-professionals . . . [It is] a masterpiece," wrote Craig Claiborne in the *New York Times.* Despite those two qualifying probablys, it is a rave. James Beard, the other titan of fine dining, wrote that he only wished he'd written it.

At the same time, Paul retired from the Foreign Service, and he and Julia moved back to the States for good, moving into a big gray clapboard house on Irving Street in Cambridge, down the street from Harvard, a town they chose for its proximity to Avis.

Alas, so much has changed since then. The average American salary was about $5,000 a year.† Gas cost twenty-five cents a gallon; a loaf of bread set you back twenty-one cents. The IBM Selectric typewriter, brand new that year, is now a relic. What hasn't changed is the way Julia's recipes still taste, the way publishing works, and the way the general public supposes it works.

Knopf, a venerable house then as now, went to great lengths to produce a beautiful book, which they then failed to promote. Even though Judith Jones, in the tradition of great editors

---

* Only the genius of acquiring editor Judith Jones assured *Mastering* did not see the light of day as The Compulsive Cook: Cooking Is My Hobby; Cooking for Love, Cook for Your Self à la Française; or any number of other horrific titles under consideration.

† $38,498 in 2012 dollars.

everywhere and for all time, was passionate about the book, Alfred Knopf himself wasn't convinced there was an enormous market for it. The house followed the time-honored tradition of tossing it into the world and seeing if anyone would buy it.*

In retrospect it seems like one day women—my mother being one—were reading and chortling over *The I Hate to Cook Book,*† throwing together the Ham-Lima Supper while mixing up a pitcher of cocktails, and the next the clouds parted and a pair of enormous dishpan hands descended from the heavens bearing a copy of *Mastering the Art of French Cooking*. But there were, in fact, plenty of cookbooks for the housewife-chauffeur or anyone else who was serious about cooking. *Gourmet's Basic French Cookbook,* by Louis Diat, the chef at New York's Ritz-Carlton, had just been published, as had Claiborne's own tome, *The New York Times Cookbook*.

Then as now, book tours were something that other authors always seemed to go on, and Julia and Simca, who'd come from France, set up their own, just as we all do today. In Chicago, Detroit, and San Francisco, they sat for interviews and did cooking demonstrations in department stores. In Pasadena, they made Roquefort quiche, fish mousse baked in a ring mold, and a Queen of Sheba chocolate cake, on a portable stove in a theater.‡

---

* The urge to reach for the "throw shit against the wall and see what sticks" analogy is nearly overwhelming, but my personal credo doesn't permit the discussion of cooking and excrement in the same paragraph, plus it would be disrespectful to Julia.

† From the introduction: "Some women, it is said, like to cook. This book is not for them." Ha!

‡ The menu is from Julia's introduction to *Mastering*. She fails to mention how they were able to bake a cake without an oven.

They repeated the same demonstration later in the afternoon. While they were in California, Julia and Paul took Simca to Disneyland. There is no record of what *La Super-Française* had to say about the Magic Kingdom or its cuisine.

The tour culminated in New York, where Julia and Simca knew exactly no one, aside from their editors at Knopf. Dione Lucas, the reigning U.S. diva of French cooking, the first female graduate of Le Cordon Bleu, who already had a few cookbooks under her belt, offered to host a dinner. Julia, who was naive in the ways of publishing, knew a thing or two about the competitive nature of chefs, and was surprised and touched by this display of generosity. Dione made filet of sole in white wine sauce, Julia and Simca prepared a boned shoulder of lamb with spinach and mushroom stuffing, and James Beard provided the guests.

Then, as now, no one was ever really sure how many copies of a book got sold. Publishers now know how many books are shipped to bookstores and Costco, but at any moment some of them may be sitting in cartons at the back of a UPS Store, on their way back to the warehouse, so the exact number is always somewhere around the number of angels you can fit on the head of a pin. *Mastering* may have sold 16,000 copies that first year, or maybe 20,000. In 1962, it was a Book-of-the-Month Club selection and snagged 35,000 copies, but BOMC printed their own, cheaper, less stupendous edition, and so once again, who knows how many "real" books sold? The book only became an "instant" bestseller forty-eight years later, after the release of *Julie & Julia,* when it sold 22,000 copies in a single week. Give or take.

As a writer, I want to say the number of people who bought and used the book matters, but the truth is that without TV Julia Child would have gone the way of, well, Simone Beck. Simca cooked, taught, and wrote books for the rest of her life,* but few people who aren't committed cooks know her name. Or the aforementioned Dione Lucas, who had not one but two cooking shows, predating Julia by a good ten years. But Lucas, whose technique was flawless, was severe and a little scary. James Beard, "The Dean of American Cookery,"† who was also a good decade ahead of Julia when it came to educating the everyday, can-opening, frozen-thawing, mix-using American-cooking ignoramuses on the deep, simple joys of making and eating good food—and who had studied acting in New York before opening a catering company, which then led to the publication of his first cookbook in 1940, *Hors d'Oeuvre and Canapés*—also couldn't quite make it on television. Like Julia, Beard was warm and charismatic, and he loved everything associated with food and cooking, but his 1946 show *I Love to Eat* suffered on several fronts. Whereas Julia would put instruction first, Beard was more interested in entertainment value: Without a moment's thought, he drew lines with blue ink in the veined Roquefort cheese to make it read better on camera and also had the makeup artist pencil in "hair" on top of his head. Then there

---

* *Simca's Cuisine* (with Patricia Simon) (1972); *New Menus from Simca's Cuisine* (with Michael James) (1979); *Food and Friends: Recipes and Memories from Simca's Cuisine* (with Suzy Patterson) (1991)

† According to the *New York Times* in 1954.

was the overacting. But a main part of his problem was simply that the time wasn't right.

But by the early sixties, the time was right. Julia simply lucked out in the way that James Beard did not. Cultural historians posit that it was because there was a French chef in the White House, or because Upper Bohemians were suddenly going to Europe, but I suspect it was the housewife/chauffeurs, the same ones who'd purchased the *I Hate to Cook Book* in droves and were sniffing around a new book called *The Feminine Mystique,** and starting to think *Now that you mention it, I hate that the highlight of my day is ironing the sheets.* Then Julia showed up with the grand, life-consuming distraction called French cooking, and the housewife/chauffeurs were, for a time, intrigued, not to say placated.

The show premiered in 1963, and by January 1965 all ninety stations on the public television network were carrying *The French Chef.* Local stores began stocking and selling out of the utensils Julia used on the show, and the *Boston Globe* called her "the talk of New England." Julia was not without her detractors. Someone concerned with hygiene criticized her for tasting with the same spoon with which she stirred, and more than one teetotaler thought there was altogether too much mention of wine, which was actually Gravy Master mixed with water.

---

* Written by Betty Friedan, and thought to be the clarion call for the second wave of feminism.

THE MIRACLE OF *THE FRENCH CHEF*

WGBH ordered three pilots of *The French Chef* in late 1962, in response to Julia's appearance on a book-chat show called *I've Been Reading*. Public television in the early 1960s was educational television, the redheaded stepchild of what would soon be called the boob tube. WGBH was so little watched that when Julia showed up to discuss *Mastering the Art of French Cooking* and, with eggs, a big copper bowl, and balloon whisk—strange implements, those—proceeded to whip up an omelet instead, the twenty-seven fan letters that "poured" into the station launched Julia to celebrity status, and the station, anxious to please those twenty-seven viewers, as well as the hundreds of others who had not written in, ordered three pilots of *The French Chef*.

At the end of her life, Julia would remember that first year of taping as being the hardest she'd every worked in her life (recall, please, the long hours she put in on The Book), taping thirty-four episodes in six months. She was paid $50 per show, which she spent mostly on ingredients.

"We're doing making your own onion soup today on *The French Chef*," Julia says, rather awkwardly, at the beginning of "Your Own French Onion Soup."

The first third of the episode is devoted to chopping onions, which can't be accomplished without the proper type of knife, honed to the proper sharpness. Julia loved her knives. She preferred an eleven-inch chef's knife of carbon steel. She looks straight into the camera to emphasize an important distinction: "People may try to tell you that the most important thing is for a knife to *hold* its edge . . . but really a good knife needs to *take* an edge." And for that she recommends basic carbon steel. Then she whips out her butcher's steel, which she loved almost as much as her knife. Then she shows us how to sharpen the knife on the steel, taking care not to "cut your hand off."

"The knife is so sharp so that when you feel it, it feels very sharp," she tells us. It's not the first time she will make absolutely no sense. And yet we are reassured. Also, a little turned on by all this knife play. There is no sawing away at the side of an onion with a dull little paring knife for Julia. Even chopping onions can be exciting, especially if you're a swashbuckler like she is.

"Knives are your life in the kitchen," she says. "You have to care for them like a baby." You must never put it in the dishwasher, or throw it into a drawer with other utensils, for fear of dulling the edge. She recommends a magnetic strip hung on the wall. The camera goes in for a close-up as she whacks the blade a little too forcefully onto the strip.

She is a little stern on the matter of onion slicing. You must learn to do it right, if you want to be serious. It may take one or two weeks to master, but you should be able to chop two to three pounds of onions in five minutes. "If you're serious about cooking, this is the dog work you should practice," she says, but then reassures us that it will all be worth it, because once you are faced with a daunting recipe for, say, French Onion Soup, that calls for about a pound of onions per person, "you'll enjoy it because it's something you enjoy and take pride in." "You'll notice I didn't cry at all," she says, triumphant. "That's because I had a great sharp knife . . . and the juice didn't splatter up in my eyes."

Perhaps more exciting than knife sharpening is cooking down the onions, then browning them, which is accomplished with half a teaspoon of sugar and a teaspoon of salt. She tips the saucepan toward the camera so we can see how those pounds of onions have shrunk to perhaps a handful of beautifully browned threads. "Look at this! It's amazing . . . That's because onions have so much water in them," she explains.

You can also spread the browned onions on steak if you want to forego the soup. "They're perfectly delicious, just the way they are."

There is a little bit of confusion over the issue of the stock. She is a firm believer in making your own stock. She suggests beef shanks, chicken necks, and carrots. "It looks awful, but it's perfectly delicious," she says as she stirs a huge pot of premade stock. She admits that if you use canned stock, you might as well just eat canned French onion soup, but she's not going to judge you for it, because then she shows you how to enhance the flavor by adding wine, herbs, and a bay leaf.

Then, you let it simmer, until, yes, it's perfectly delicious.

After she's demonstrated making the "croutes" from a loaf of French bread, and shows how to grate some Swiss cheese into the soup to make it extra stringy, the camera suddenly pans up to the ceiling—whoops!—while Julia, now offscreen, goes about her business demonstrating how to make individual bowls, with their own single croute, grated cheese, and if you're extra hungry (and hoping to have a heart attack that very day), a poached egg. She then moves to the oven and pulls the casserole from the broiler, where the cheese has been browning. "It's so hot, I better not forget to use pot holders," she says to herself, and there's a brief, harrowing moment where it looks as if she might dump the whole thing on her shoes. She places it on the counter, and from our angle, it looks blackened, not browned. "It's possibly browned too much," she trills, "but it gives a good effect!"

She then takes the casserole into the dining room next door. It's important to serve the soup hot, right at the table, with a big ladle. The table is long and narrow, and when Julia sits down, we can really see how tall she is. This soup is hardy enough to serve with only a green salad, and some nice Beaujolais, or "California Mountain Red." She reassures us that this is a sensational meal, and then comes the moment that seals the deal, that causes us to bond with this strange cooking teacher now and forever: She leans toward the camera and confides, "When you've added all those French touches, who's going to know?"

Do not apologize.
Who's going to know? That simple, rhetorical aside revolutionized American cooking more surely than did any of the French terms or techniques that Julia was so determined to convey. She

was saying, in essence, that this cooking you're doing? *It's for you.* You're expected to feed the family anyway, so why not take charge of it in a way that doesn't make you feel like an indentured servant, but more like an artist? Why not enjoy yourself, give yourself a sense of achievement and pride, and feel good about what you've made? This is where the cooking moved from something done in the name of service, to something done to satisfy and enrich the cook. Don't apologize, and if something falls on the floor, pick it up. So important is this having fun, feeling good and proud and accomplished, that you mustn't fret if things aren't perfect because *Who's going to know?*

The greatest contribution Coco Chanel made to modern style was not the insistence on simple lines, or the invention of the cardigan or the little black dress, but the notion that a woman is most beautiful when she feels comfortable in her clothes. Prior to Chanel, it was all about how good you looked from ten paces. It mattered not whether the fabric was stiff and scratchy, the raw seams poked you, the waist was so tight you lived in a constant state of having stars before your eyes: Beauty was always in the eye of the beholder.

Likewise, Julia turned the drudgery of cooking on its ear.* Her message was a double threat. First, she insisted that things be done properly, with attention to detail. Unlike the magazine and book editors who disparaged the ability of housewives to do, well, pretty much anything, so timid were they, so afraid of

---

* The argument could be made that she raised the bar, and I've made it, but that came later.

challenge or difficulty,* Julia had confidence that if her viewers were "serious," they could master what she had to teach them. In the same way that a mother bestows confidence on her child by assuming he's up to the task of say, getting his science project completed and in on time, Julia granted us the confidence to do it because she knew we could.

Second, she knew that mastering anything was a process, and just because you were serious, that didn't mean you wouldn't mess up, a lot. Her own show is a real-time lesson on this philosophy: the nonsensical instructions, the occasions when things are overdone or underdone, or something that's supposed to adhere, doesn't. This is simply the way of it, or so the unspoken message goes, and there's no need to apologize, *ever*.

This was an attitude she adopted after she'd been at the Cordon Bleu for only a few weeks. She made eggs Florentine for a friend, neglecting to measure the flour and substituting chicory for spinach, proclaiming them afterwards to be the most "vile eggs Florentine I have ever imagined could be made outside of England." You didn't apologize because it put the guest in the uncomfortable position of having to lie to reassure you, but you also didn't apologize because this was just part of the rigors and challenge of cooking: Sometimes it just didn't work out and there was nothing for it.

By the time Julia became The French Chef, she had finally figured out her audience. The "servantless American cook" that

---

* Given all this impairment, why anyone would marry them is a mystery.

she, Simca, and Louisette had arrived on sort of haphazardly as their target audience had morphed first into the mythic loathsome housewife/chauffeur and finally "into a readership that not simply enjoys cooking, but was also excited by the challenge of making something fabulous and difficult, the effort made more seductive still by the fact it was French." This was the person she was addressing when she looked into the camera.

For all of the equality feminism has wrought, women are still the Apologizing Gender. Not long ago I did an inventory on how often I apologized for something. For a week I wrote down everything I said I was sorry for. I don't especially consider myself someone who's eager to please. Around our house, which is now just Jerrod and me, my daughter having gone off to college, I do pretty much exactly what I want. I do laundry when I feel the need to do something that occupies my hands and not my mind, make the bed most, but not all, mornings, cook when I feel like it, order out when I don't. If I'm really feeling wild, I go outside and prune the roses and tug a weed. As my own boss, I'm never late for meetings, never fail to get the memo, or send one for that matter, and I have no one but myself to answer to when I screw up. I meet friends for drinks or for a walk when the mood strikes; Jerrod and I grab a movie when the spirit moves us, or go for rides on his motorcycle. Sometimes, we borrow his parents' RV and head out somewhere where we can ride horses. My major day-to-day obligation is feeding the dogs.

You would think someone with this much agency would not have so much for which to apologize. These were the things I was sorry for, that week:

- Answering an e-mail late (it had been three days)

- Walking out of the library with a book that I thought I'd checked out but hadn't (an honest mistake)

- Taking the trash cans to the street for garbage pickup and not lining them up so that it was easy to back out of the driveway (a little lazy, but look who was taking out the trash)

- While playing World of Warcraft, failing to reapply Blessing of Might, thus making it more difficult for Jerrod's Druid tank to hold aggro (everybody died)

- Being less than five minutes late meeting a friend for a coffee ("I'm sorry!" by which I mean, "Hey, how are you?")

- Accidentally making some garlic bread with butter and ginger paste instead of garlic paste (Ugh, sorry)

- Texting at dinner (justified)

- Sneezing (I said excuse me, a form of "I'm sorry")

Why all this apologizing? Except for the texting, which admittedly was rude, I had nothing to apologize for. It's a terrible and silly tic, and it's not remotely polite. Instead, it creates the mental habit of feeling apologetic.

I don't doubt that Julia apologized when she was wrong. Part of her upbringing as an Upper Middle Brow–girl in Pasadena would have dictated that she had good manners, but she was not about to apologize when she'd done nothing wrong. One could argue that failing to measure the flour in that long-ago eggs Florentine was "wrong," but mastering cooking—or anything—is a process to be both accepted and respected, and the people who benefit from your practice—your friends and family—must also accept and respect it.

There is no need to reinvent yourself.
If you are old enough to have watched *The French Chef* as a child, it's nearly impossible to watch it today free of the miasma of nostalgia. The perky vintage 1960s theme music.* The grainy black-and-white film. The often lame introduction. (Who can forget "These are the chicken sisters!") Front and center, Julia herself, wearing her uniform of cotton-blouse-with-strange-badge,† pearls, and apron tied at the front.

I set my college-age daughter down to watch some Julia, to see if it resonated. She doesn't watch any of those chef

---

* Composed by John Morris, who worked mostly with Mel Brooks, and who also composed the music for *Dirty Dancing*, which was also set, ironically, in 1963, the same year *The French Chef* premiered.

† She faithfully wore the École des Gourmandes badge from the little cooking school she had with Simca and Louisette in her attic kitchen on the Roo de Loo. I don't think anyone knew what it was for years.

shows—Master, Iron, or Top—or *Cake Boss,* or *Kelsey's Essentials,* or that show with Paula Deen's son. The entire food-show phenomenon—spawned, of course, by the success of *The French Chef*—holds no interest for her, at least not yet.

She watched the quiche episode and was surprised. "Julia is so natural and normal," she said. "I felt like I was in the kitchen with her. I wanted to be in the kitchen with her!"

Julia's ability to be herself in front of the camera hypnotized us, and still does, apparently. Who was this large, occasionally breathless, excitable woman who had no ability to put on airs? It wasn't as if she forgot the camera was there—every once in a while, especially in the early episodes, she looks up and into it with a startled smile—but she possessed no ability to alter behavior because it *was* there. She would sometimes crack herself up and do nothing to disguise her glee. In the episode on how to roast a chicken, when describing the age of an old stewing hen, she said, "This chicken is beyond the age of consent" and practically laughed out loud at her own improvisation. Each show was filmed in one take, and some were rougher than others. The aforementioned "To Roast a Chicken" was particularly rocky. The sentence "This chicken weighs five and a half to nine months" was followed moments later with information on how much you might expect to spend: "It's twice as much more expensiver than."

Viewers not only didn't mind her mistakes, they loved them and found them comforting. They loved watching her taste something. She lowered her eyelids, her gaze softened, then she slurped or licked or bit. She was somewhere else, focused within, feeling the food in her mouth, evaluating it, reflecting upon what needed to change. We were transfixed.

Even though TV was in its toddlerhood, viewers could still smell a phony. It's what sunk James Beard, who misread the medium and believed that showmanship and being "entertaining" was all that was required. WGBH was besieged with fan mail raving about Julia's "honesty," "forthrightness," "naturalness," "lack of that TV manner."

The obvious lesson here is to "be yourself" just like Julia was, but the degree to which that's easier said than done cannot be underestimated. For one thing Julia, because of her staggering height and unusual voice, had, from a very young age, no choice but to be herself. There was no radar beneath which she could fly, no opportunity for her, ever, to adopt the affectations of a conventional woman and get away with it. Who she was, was who she had to be; when the camera was turned on her at the age of fifty, she had no experience being anyone else.

This isn't true for most of us. Most of us fit in better than Julia did, and the pernicious urge, from the time we are small, day in day out, week in week out, in order to keep fitting in, is to succumb to the society-pleasing parts of our personalities. Most of the time you think, Where's the harm in acting more accommodating than I really am? Or feigning an interest in soccer or locally grown produce that I don't really possess? Or pretending to be superinvolved in my kids' enrichment activities? Or overpaying for a pair of low-rise jeans that don't really fit, aren't comfortable, and prevent me from sitting on a bar stool without my ass hanging out? Or laughing more than is entirely necessary at that hot guy's joke? And speaking of being hot, as long as you're able to work your hotness every waking moment, you're exempt from everything listed above.*

My point is that the average woman's inclination to obey her culture's imperatives is a tiny, constant stream that eventually creates a majestic, postcard-worthy canyon of *Who the hell am I?* And if, perchance, you've decided you're alternative and edgy, with a snarky blog, chipped dark brown nail polish, and a fashion pieced together from the thirteen cents a pound bin at the Goodwill, you're fighting the same losing battle. Sorry.

All this said, usually by age fifty—Julia's age when those first pilots were filmed—if we're ever going to figure out who we really are, now is the time. We've lived a little, have accepted that we're never going to go to the Olympics in any sport other than dressage or shooting, and that we do, in fact, have a favorite child.

And what does society, by which I mean women's magazines and the *Huffington Post,* think we should do just as our real personality is throwing aside its chains? Reinvent ourselves.

Do not reinvent yourself, that's the lesson behind this section. Reinvention is code word for using all your God-given

---

* Except, obviously, the low-rise jeans. The alternative to low-rise jeans are the heinous, hateful mom jeans. A woman in mom jeans, even if she is a mom, is the most pathetic creature to walk the earth. Whoever is the current Sexiest Woman Alive, were she to don a pair of mom jeans, would instantly become a frightful hag.

brute female mojo—your intuition, perception, stamina, resilience, wisdom, and perhaps cash from your IRA—to do something so new, your personality has to be taken down to the studs and rebuilt. Give up your job as head of human resources at that Fortune 500 company and open that dude ranch in Wyoming. Give up teaching cha-cha to seniors and go to law school. Close your law practice and move to Cambodia, where you do something or other with children. What you are doing here is disrespecting all of your hard-won experience and knowledge and turning yourself back into a beginner, a neophyte, someone with "girlish" enthusiasm, but no expertise.

If you're over, say, forty, you know some things. Citing the accomplishments of Bill Gates and the Beatles, Malcolm Gladwell, in his book *Outliers,* posits that it takes practicing for 10,000 hours to become an expert. Why throw away what you've become at least good enough at to be a newbie at something else? Even though it sounds all life-affirming and proactive, it feels like just one more case of discouraging women from owning who they are. And if there's any doubt, consider that reinvention is not something pressed on men.

I'm not saying you shouldn't make a change; be Julia, and slide into something challenging and novel, but not completely out of your wheelhouse.

Julia, on TV, was the sum of all of the Julias she had been: the popular girl in high school; the crazy college roommate; the emperor on stage, hamming it up; the dizzy newlywed hurling herself into Parisian culture and French cuisine; the cookbook writer; the scientist and educator. When she first saw herself on camera, she was appalled, calling herself Mrs. Steam Engine. She was always trying to improve her ability to move around the set, explain the steps while handling the ingredients, and make eye contact with the camera. Notes from producers said things like "Stop gasping" and "Wipe brow," but no one ever suggested she do anything that wasn't in keeping with who she was.

Find yourself a Paul Child.
The French Chef, which aired nationally through 1973, first in black and white and then in color (the ubiquitous mid-gray-toned cotton blouse was revealed to be a nice French blue), only *wished* it had had a shoestring on which to be produced. The budget pretty much consisted of the money to pay the light bill. Each show took roughly nineteen hours of pre-production, which consisted of Julia and Paul at home in their kitchen, breaking down each recipe into individual movements and points of instruction, which he would then time with his stopwatch. If Julia felt she needed diagrams to better explain herself, Paul would stay up until the wee hours, rendering something that could have hung in a museum. His drawing of the four stomachs of the cow for the *Tripes à la Mode* episode is particularly nice.

On the day of taping, the Childs arose at 6:00 a.m. It was winter in Boston, so you know how much fun getting out of that warm bed must have been. The Cambridge Electric Company display kitchen, where the episodes were shot, was on the second floor of the building, and Paul shoveled the snow off the fire escape before lugging in the pots and pans they'd brought from their own kitchen. (Easier, apparently, than taking the building's freight elevator.) There were no production assistants, no gofers, no interns. There was Paul, and whatever grip or gaffer was standing around the Cambridge Electric Company's display kitchen with nothing to do. After the taping, the crew would eat, while Paul did the dishes.

Reader, I wish I could offer concrete advice on how to find and land your own Paul Child, a guy who will effortlessly switch roles with you if and when your career suddenly takes off, becoming in a matter of a few short months the wife to you that you once were to him, but I fear it's mostly a matter of luck.

Rule <u>No.</u> 9:
Make the World Your Oyster (Stew)

⚜

Toujours Bon Appétit.

The episodes of *The French Chef* that I watched with my mother were only slightly more interesting than the 1968 presidential returns and, a few years later, the Watergate hearings, except for one episode, which I recall in detail: Julia Child's *Reine de Saba* (Queen of Sheba) Cake. I'm sure it's because it had the word cake in the title. I remember Julia cautioning us to make sure we had everything we needed before we began baking, and placing all the ingredients on a special tray, leveling the cup of flour with the back edge of the knife, and checking to see if the cake was done using a toothpick.* But my clearest

------

* How weird was that? My dad used a toothpick after dinner, while he sat and drank his coffee and read the paper.

memory occurs after the show is over, when my mother sighed loudly and flipped her steno book closed with an expression of dissatisfaction I couldn't name. "Maybe we could make that!" I said. "We don't *bake*," she replied, then lit a cigarette and blew two streams of smoke through her nose. We don't? All that grocery shopping she did, all that recipe clipping, all that menu planning, all those dinners that took hours to prepare and we didn't *bake*? Then I thought a little more and realized that she was right. The Van de Kamp's oatmeal cookies I was always trying to sneak were store bought, and so was my birthday cake.

Now I was interested.

In the movie version, at this moment there would be a smash cut to me, decades later, a grown woman, standing in my kitchen with a 7UP bottle inside a flour-covered tube sock, expertly rolling out the pastry dough for my much-celebrated lattice-top blackberry pie. I make one or two blackberry pies a week starting in early July, the week marionberries are available at the local farmers' market.

A cross between the Chehalem and the Olallie berry, the Marion was cultivated at Oregon State University in 1956 and is considered the "cabernet of blackberries" for its complex taste, both sweet and earthy. It's perfectly delicious, as Julia would say, and I prefer it to all other blackberries for my pies. I love making pies, because unlike whatever that thing is you've got stirring in the saucepan, a pie is a beautiful self-contained object that no one really needs, but that everyone, when presented with one, is delighted to have. When it comes to pies I'm not a Flimsie, and over the years I've developed the sort of seriousness about pie making of which Julia would approve. Baking one makes me tremble with joy.

The second thing I like to make, and which I am expert at making, is Julia's Tarte Tatin, invented many years ago by the Tatin sisters in Lamotte-Beuvron, their restaurant in the Loire Valley. It's a tricky and thrilling dish to pull off, because you construct it upside down, caramelizing the sliced apples on the stove top in a cast-iron skillet, then covering it with pastry dough. After baking it right in the skillet, you haul that baby out of the oven, flip it over onto a big plate, and if you've done it right, everything holds together, and the apples, once on the bottom, are now on top, a glistening rich brown. I make Tarte Tatins all fall, stopping only when I can no longer zip up my jeans.

I know a thing or two about making Julia's Tarte Tatin, as does Kathy, who also considers herself an expert on the matter, and when Marcelline, our own *Super-Française,* finally granted us permission to use her oven, we decided that we must make one.

That day, once again, it was dreary and raining, and before we left our apartment the neighbor was already shrieking her head off. Who was she yelling at? The poor dog? The young lover she had chained to the hot water pipe? The deformed mother in the wheelchair? No one? The morning of the Tarte Tatin was especially dramatic. When we stood with our ears to the wall the only words we understood were "fucking fucking shit." Also, the Brie de Meaux we'd gaily purchased the day of our arrival was beginning to stink to high heaven, but we couldn't bring ourselves to be typically American and throw it out. We were both in a mood.

Marcelline has a small apartment in a high-rise in the 19th, one of the outlying arrondissements where everyday Parisians live, not far from the Parc des Buttes Chaumont, the big, hilly park where Napoleon planted all the exotic trees he could get his hands on—Siberian elms, lindens, ginkos, giant sequoias, and a few cedars of Lebanon.

Marcelline is tiny and brilliant, an English teacher and writer, and inasmuch as any French person falls into the food-as-fuel camp, she does. Her small, neat kitchen is equipped with only the basics; no million-dollar E. Dehillerin copper pots for her.

During most of our time in Paris, I was Kathy's sous chef, mostly because a lot of what we cooked fell firmly in the sauté-ing/simmering/deglazing realm of my mother, and thus it was less interesting to me. But the Tarte Tatin was my territory.

Together we made the pastry dough, peeled and sliced the apples. She then arranged them in a pattern at the bottom of the skillet in the butter and sugar and dropped the circle of pastry dough on top.

"Wait!" I cried. "What about the caramelizing?"

"It happens when it bakes," she said.

"You need to cook it on the stove first, before you put on the dough."

"What are you talking about?"

"You cook it on the stove first, and baste it with the butter."

"This is the way Julia does it," she said.

"No, Julia cooks it on the stove first, then puts it in the oven."

"No, she doesn't!"

"Yes, she does!" I cried. A week before we came here I made two Tarte Tatins, and after you arrange the apples in the pan, you baste the apples with the butter to get it to caramelize before it goes in the oven. I'm *positive* "

Kathy is half-Serbian and half-Albanian and is much more stubborn than I am, but I knew I was right, and she saw my certainty, and then said, "Well, I'm doing it my way," and slid the skillet into the oven.

"But you can't do it your way!" I shouted. "The whole reason we're here is to cook Julia and this isn't Julia cooking, it's your cooking!"

"I've done it this way for years."

"You can't!"

"I'm doing it this way."

"Well I'm the one writing the book, and I'm going to use your real name."*

The Tarte turned out perfectly delicious, if a little pale, *because it was under-caramelized,* which made complete sense, since if you just throw it in the oven without monitoring the tricky caramelization process, you're just baking on a wing and

---

* It's Kathy Budas.

a prayer, something of which Julia would never approve. Later, because I couldn't let it go, I did some research and discovered that in fact both methods were "Julia"; Kathy was making the Tarte Tatin from *Mastering*, and I was used to the recipe from *The Way To Cook,** which is, according to Julia, the fourth iteration of the recipe, and, in her opinion, the final and correct one.

That night we took the Tarte Tatin back to the apartment. I held the plate on my lap in the Metro and was disappointed that no one commented on it. I was disappointed in general, because it turned out that cooking Julia was no guarantee that you would be infused with the magic of being Julia. We were just two old friends in Paris squabbling over how to bake a Tarte.

But when we turned onto rue de l'Exposition, we almost ran into our neighbor, out walking her dog. She was tall but thin and wore a short, chic brown wig. We'd caught her placing something just inside the gate at the Romanian embassy. We pretended to window-shop, looking with feigned interest at the shampoo on display in the Confidence beauty salon, waiting for her to go inside. Once she did, we ran across the street, careful not to drop our Tarte Tatin, to see what she'd left. It was a can of Ocean Spray Cranberry Sauce.

So absurd was this, we forgot our argument, went upstairs, and devoured the tart straight out of the baking dish.

----

* page 435, see *Preliminary Stove-Top Cooking*

FANFARE FOR THE MIDDLE-AGED WOMAN

By 1966, Julia was *it*. That year she won an Emmy and appeared on the cover of *Time* magazine. The illustration showed Julia with redder hair than she'd probably had in thirty years, surrounded by her glimmering copper pots; beneath her chin is a plate of some kind of cartoon-looking fish with orange spots, displayed on a bed of something green. "The Lady with the Ladle," they called her, and saluted her for single-handedly rescuing Americans from their wretched Miracle Whip salads and gloppy frozen chicken pot pies.

The celebration of Julia as The One was simplistic and inaccurate. Julia's friend M.F.K. Fisher had been writing about fine dining and gastronomy since the 1930s, *Gourmet* magazine had been around since 1941, and James Beard, while not a French cook, was a believer in all the things Julia championed: taking your time, cooking with love, having a care for the outcome. Craig Claiborne, who'd trained in French haute cuisine in Lausanne, Switzerland, and who brought major food coverage to the nation's paper of record, had been reviewing cookbooks and restaurants, and writing columns about fine dining for years.

Still, none of them were Julia.

There is possibly no better middle-aged woman in twentieth-century history than Julia Child. That's what *Time* magazine should have celebrated her for. Compared with the mundane yet agonizing minute-to-minute struggles of the regular fifty-four-year-old woman—her age when she was crowned Our

Lady of the Ladle—anyone can write a three-pound cookbook and film thirty-four television episodes in a single take over a six-month period, not to mention cook for her husband every night of the Lord. (You didn't think Paul grilled up his own lamb chops, did you?)

And speaking of Julia's apple tarts, in an early episode of *The French Chef,** watch the first few minutes, and you will see a close-up on Julia's hands as she prepares the pastry crust, measuring out the flour and cutting in the cold butter. Do you see those spots on her hands? Those are age spots, Reader. And yet, there are her capable hands, working away, and her voice tootles and trills offscreen above them. Her hands have age spots, and yet Julia still thinks what she has to say has merit.

I'm willing to believe that this wasn't so astounding in the mid-1960s. For one thing, Tina Fey hadn't yet made the observation that in Hollywood older women (thirty-nine and up) are considered crazy because "the definition of crazy in show business is a woman who keeps talking even after no one wants to fuck her anymore."

I want to say Fey's observation wasn't true in Julia's day, or if it was no one admitted it. I want to say, "In Julia's day people had more respect for their elders," but Julia was so long-lived— she lived to be ninety-one, dying in her sleep two days before

---

* Called, nonsensically, French Tarts, Apple Style. Shouldn't it be Apple Tarts, French Style?

her ninety-second birthday*—it would be unclear the "day" to which I'm referring. Also, I remember a moment in 1968, in Laguna Beach, where we had a beach house for a time, when my father, having just come from work in his shirt and tie, was spit on by some hippies sitting on the sidewalk in front of a juice bar, and that's not very respectful now, is it? But I won't say those things because it's the twenty-first century now, and anytime a woman references the past, she renders herself instantly irrelevant. Is this also true for men? I don't know. Somewhere they have their own apologist tackling this issue.

Julia, the Best Middle-Aged Woman Ever, at least had the advantage of being famous during a time when being middle-aged wasn't considered an embarrassing display of bad character worthy of shunning. Being an adult was still something to which children and teenagers aspired. Did they sit at the feet of their elders seeking wisdom? Of course not, but they saw that becoming an adult was a prison break. To be an adult meant staying up as late as you wanted, ignoring your chores, spending

---

* One of the most depressing parts about writing about someone's life is that sometime during the last chapters you have to say she died. And while death might be one of life's realities, we builders of narratives can choose to downplay it. A week before her death in Montecito, California, in the summer of 2002, Julia was still working on her memoir *My Life in France* with her great-nephew, Alex Prud'homme, a task she adored because, she said, Alex reminded her so much of Paul. When she died in her sleep on August 13, 2004, two days before her birthday, the party went on as planned, and people arrived from around the world to drink and eat and celebrate. There. Now let's not speak about it again.

your money as you pleased, not having to wash your face and brush your teeth, and, best of all, getting stoned without having to roll up a towel and stuff it beneath the door.

Now, because everyone from toddlerhood on up is allowed not only to do whatever they please, but also encouraged to do so in the name of "being who they are,"* middle-aged people rightly see that life is much better when you're underaged and your skin is rudely smooth, your torso is a taut, flexible stem, and your parents are still footing the bill. When you walk through the world, people admire you for being young and free, consumed with texting and hooking up. No one gazes upon the average fifty-year-old and admires her for supporting those children, for making sure there's food in the house and on the table, and, possibly, for paying for that house. Wisdom is merely the consolation prize for aging. One could go on, but of course, in going on, one just reaffirms one's status as a crazy woman in "mid-life," the new euphemism for middle-age that's meant to sound more like an expensive blue jean than the depressing reminder of mortality that it is.

No one told Julia that middle-aged women weren't allowed to hog the spotlight, or that if they did, they could only do it if they passed as someone much younger. Maybe it was all that time spent in Europe, where women aren't rendered instantly irrelevant at the first hot flash, or maybe it was because Julia was

---

* Just yesterday a friend, a mother of four children under the age of eleven, said that she and her husband believed the best parenting was "getting out of the way" and just allowing her kids to "be."

never the prettiest girl in the class, or even one of the pretty ones. "I learned the truth at seventeen/that love was meant for beauty queens," Janis Ian crooned in 1975. The song won a Grammy and went on to top the billboard charts. Why? Because every record-buying girl between the ages of six and twenty-six knew this to be the Painful Truth of Life.

Except, it isn't. Because one of the secrets of life, hiding there in plain sight, is that we're "old," i.e., not seventeen or eighteen or even twenty-two, for a very long time. So-called "mid-life" is the Sahara Desert of the human life span. It goes on for decades. If, like Julia, you were never a beauty queen—and who among us was, really? Consumer culture conspires to make sure pretty much every woman feels bad about her neck (thighs, hips, waist, hair, nose, lips, philtrum*)—middle-age is the great equalizer. The older you get, the less the great female currency of youth and beauty is worth. Trying to look like a hot twentysomething when you're fifty is the modern woman's comb-over: No one is fooled. Indeed, if you did not spend your formative years as a smokin' hot babe, where the world was your oyster simply because you happened to be born with good looks, middle-age is for you.

All you women who suffered for having "great personalities," please step forward.

Julia did, wielding her eccentric personality and *joie de vivre* like the fright knife she waved over her head on *The French Chef.*

Middle-age was the time of Julia's life.

---

* The groove that runs between your nose and lip.

STILL, IT'S GOOD TO LOOK GOOD

It was never easy for Julia to find clothes that suited her. Her height limited her fashion options; no jeans or fetchingly sloppy boyfriend cardigan for Julia. Until the end of her life, her style read "woman." She wore skirts, blouses, and her famous pearls. In a little seen black-and-white photo taken just after the publication of *Mastering,* she's wearing what appears to be a classic Chanel suit with bouclé jacket and iconic Chanel hat.

The early episodes of *The French Chef* are so dear because Julia looks like exactly what she was, a slightly frazzled home cook with flat hair in the back of her head and bags under her eyes. Dissatisfied with the way she looked, she realized quickly that if you wanted to succeed in this new medium, you better look good.

She didn't wear much makeup, believing that her eyes weren't made for mascara, and solved the problem in a rather badass fashion with plastic surgery.

She had an "eye job" in the late 1960s. In 1971 she had a face-lift, and another in 1977, and yet another in 1989. The last one made her look like someone wearing a Julia Child rubber mask, but she was determined to stay in it as long as possible, and she knew viewers would prefer to learn to cook from someone fresh and vital-looking, than from an old bag with one foot in the grave.

For Julia, to give up on her looks meant to give up on living life to its fullest, and if it took a plastic surgeon's knife, then so be it.

WHEN THE HITS JUST KEEP ON COMING

In addition to the basic indignities of aging, the strange fore-arm flab where no fat exists, the suddenly chubby armpits and propensity for weeping at the National Anthem, life tends to get deadly serious, fast. It happens to us all, and it happened to Julia.

The first hit came in May 1962, while she and Paul were preparing to film *The French Chef* pilot episodes. John McWilliams Jr., Julia's cantankerous right-wing father, died. He was eighty-two, suffered from myriad ailments—a pesky virus, emphysema, perhaps leukemia—and the end was prolonged enough so that Julia could fly from Cambridge to Pasadena for the bedside vigil. She had dutifully written Pop a weekly letter while she and Paul lived abroad, and she sent him clippings and updates about her doings once *Mastering* had been published to acclaim. She'd never failed to send the yearly birthday and Christmas cards. It had never mattered. Her marriage to Paul, whom Pop found to be beneath contempt, as an intellectual and thus a communist, had sundered him from his daughter forever.

Julia's sadness was tempered, as always, by the pragmatism that drove her character. If her father had lived to be a hundred and two there was never going to be a chance of reconciliation, something she'd managed to make peace with long ago. She was grateful Pop had enjoyed a happy second marriage, and that his death was mercifully quick. Except when it came to finding the proper casings with which to stuff a homemade *saucisson,* or whether it was okay to substitute cream for butter, Julia never overthought anything, and we are well-advised to do the same. She was saddened but was able to move on.

Then, a scant six years later, in 1968, while she and Simca were pushing to finish *Mastering the Art of French Cooking, Volume Two,* she discovered a lump in her left breast. The cancer wasn't life-threatening, and the same diagnosis today would call for a lumpectomy. "Left breast off," she wrote in her diary on February 28. The surgeon removed her lymph nodes, too. The surgery required a ten-day hospital stay, during which Paul, a lifelong hypochondriac, nearly required hospitalization himself. It is said that when it was over, Julia wept in private.*

Even in these times, when open heart surgery is practically an outpatient procedure, ten days in the hospital is a long time for the average person; may we stop for a moment and meditate on just how long that must have been for Julia, who was, let's be honest, a manic workaholic?

Her recovery was not as speedy as she might have wished. She had to wear a plastic sleeve on the left arm and spend time getting outfitted with "a false titty," as she confided to a friend. Cooking was difficult, but she felt lucky it wasn't her right arm; *that* might have really tripped her up. She was anxious to get back to work on *Volume Two,* and at her weekly post-op doctor's appointment, her only question was, When could she return to France?

---

* Which does beg the question, if it was in private how could anyone be sure?

Find your passion.

One of the standard-issue life lessons, which I'm sure I've posited along with everyone else who thinks about these things, is that one's life is enriched immeasurably if you're able to find an abiding passion. You don't have to be good at it, it just has to be something that would consume every waking hour if you let it. A good friend, a New York book editor, discovered surfing in her forties and now spends her vacations at a house she built in Costa Rica, and on the weekends, at her apartment in Manhattan, she gets lost in surfing movies, videos, and books. The walls of her office are adorned with big pictures of cresting waves.

There is another, less often mentioned, advantage to possessing a lifelong passion: When you're getting on in years and your parents are dying, and your body is reminding you in the least dignified manner possible that it, too, will fail you sometime, perhaps in the not too distant future, having something you care about deeply gives you hope, focus, and a reason not to dwell on the bad stuff. We don't discuss this much, I think, because what could be more of a downer? *Find your passion! It'll keep you from jumping off a bridge when you're middle-aged!* But a deep passion for something outside yourself is money in the bank.

In drawing up the contract for *Volume Two,* Julia's editor, Judith Jones, suggested Julia and Simca include a recipe for French bread, which Americans simply could not find even in so-called French bakeries. The ingredients are flour, yeast, water, and salt. What could be easier? Everything, as it turns out.

After spending two years producing pale, gummy loaves at home, Julia went to Paris and apprenticed herself to French bread-making expert Raymond Calvel. "It was like the sun in all his glory, breaking through the shades of gloom," she would later write in her Foreword to *Volume Two*. Calvel set her on the right path. Paul took pictures of his hands at work. Back home in Cambridge, they were able to copy Calvel's moves, but alas, not the necessary dampness in his baker's oven.

Julia dubbed Paul "M. Paul Beck, Boulanger" after he got into the act, baking his own loaves, experimenting with how much and what kind of yeast to use, how best to get the dough to rise and for how long, how large the loaf should be, and how to moisten it while it was baking. M. Paul Beck squirted the top of the baking bread with the sprayer appropriated from his nasal decongestant, and Julia used a wet whisk broom. They made *baguettes* (translated as "the stick"), *batards* (half the size of a baguette), *flutes* (twice the size of a baguette), and *ficelles* (a glorified bread stick that must be eaten as soon as it comes out of the oven, or else risk breaking a tooth). They would nail the recipe, leap around with glee, then discover they couldn't duplicate it. Two hundred and eighty-four pounds of white flour later, Julia felt confident she'd mastered *Pain Français.** It was this kind of dedication and enthusiasm that kept her grounded and optimistic about the future.

---

* The recipe is seventeen pages long. You owe it to yourself to bake it, just to appreciate the sheer lunacy it must have taken to perfect it.

I often wonder whether Julia ever experienced any dark nights of the soul. Paul was pretty much all dark nights, all the time, pessimistic and fretful and prone to depression. Did she ever sit in her kitchen with a cigarette—yes, she was a heavy smoker until after her mastectomy—and a glass of Beaujolais and remember her beloved mother, Caro, who died at sixty, not young, but certainly not old, and how she, Julia, with a bout of breast cancer behind her was only a few years younger? Did she think, I better make the most of this because who knows what the future holds, and wallowing about anything is pointless and a waste of time?

If at all possible, build an adorable vacation home in the south of France.
With Julia's first two royalty checks* she and Paul built a small house in Provence, on the corner of a plot of land owned for generations by the family of Jean Fischbacher, Simca's husband, and where Simca and Jean lived in a three-story house made of stone. Plascassier is a small village on the winding road between Valbonne and Grasse. For Julia, it was heaven: She was in France, yet the diffused golden light, the rolling green-gray hills, the smell of jasmine, orange blossom, and lavender in the air, reminded her of her California. It was possibly the most perfect place imaginable: a place that evokes all the glorious

---

* Totaling about $45,000; about $388,500 in 2012 dollars.

aspects of childhood, without the attendant traumatic reminders lurking in the actual place you grew up. For Paul it was perfect because he got to build a house to his specifications, using his flawless French.

The small house, called "La Pitchoune," which Paul and Julia, those compulsive nicknamers, immediately re-dubbed La Peetch, was more or less a kitchen and a bedroom—Paul and Julia each had their own; Julia was a prodigious snorer—plus a living room. Then as now,* the kitchen is warm but not fancy, with slightly higher counters and the cream-colored pegboard with its black utensil outlines, and a fine collection of copper pots.

Outside, on the terrace, they built a concrete patio table that resembled a mushroom. "You could get the measure of someone's character, sitting at that table," Julia used to say.

James Beard was someone whose character Julia approved of, and he visited her often in Provence. She never forgot the generosity he showed her upon the publication of *Mastering,* and even though they championed different cuisines, Julia and Jim shared the belief that nothing was more fun than working hard in the kitchen, and that making good food was not only endlessly interesting but also life's highest calling. Beard was also fun and forgiving. Once, in Cambridge, when they were first

---

* Kathie Alex, a onetime student of Simca's, lives there now and runs a summer cooking program called Cooking in France with Friends.

becoming friendly and Julia was enjoying Famous Cookbook Author status, she cooked him a terrible meal of flavorless veal scallops, underdone broccoli, and dusty-tasting chocolate cake, which he shrugged off with a laugh and an invitation to cook at his school. He descended on La Peetch the summer of 1969, where together they watched the moon landing.

The great advantage (and disadvantage) of living a stone's throw away from Simca was living a stone's throw away from Simca. Paul and Julia lived most of the year in Cambridge but spent the winter months in Provence.

Because Julia had been right on that awkward day in Boston when she tried to convince the people of Houghton Mifflin that cooking French food could fill several volumes, Julia and Simca had plenty of recipes to fill *Volume Two*. They restored some of the sauces and chicken recipes edited from Volume One, included more soups, bisques, and fish stews, and more vegetable recipes, including the "American vegetable" broccoli, of which Julia was quite fond, and more desserts, which were Simca's specialty.

Fifteen years, give or take, had passed since Julia and Simca had met in Paris. They were not just older but significantly wiser, especially when it came to the highly specialized task of writing a cookbook of French recipes for American cooks. They'd made it up as they went along the first time around; now, with one book behind them, Julia was very clear about what worked and what didn't and what needed to change. Her inner scientist was more finicky than ever. She demanded more operational proof than ever, particularly when it came to using American ingredients, which had turned out to be more than a little different from those found in France. American flour had more gluten than French flour; American chocolate had more butter fat; American sole filets were thicker; American chickens tasted "less chickeny." This made a huge difference, and she and Simca would have to make sure to allow for these differences. On and on it went. Julia was a mad researching fool, more obsessed than ever about why and how recipes *worked.*

Simca was intuitive and improvisational. Most of their original recipes came from her family, and she could make them in her sleep. Julia had the considerably more complex task of interpreting Simca's instructions for herself, then re-cooking the dish with American ingredients, then writing the recipe in a way that an American cook could follow, *then* presenting the dish to Simca for her "approval," which rarely happened, because even though the original recipe had, say, required leeks, Simca had decided that maybe leeks were not such a good idea after all, and so Julia would return to her kitchen to remake the dish with no leeks. They were the Lennon-McCartney of cookery: For several halcyon years their differences combined to create an unprecedented work of genius, but those same differences guaranteed that it could never last.

Julia loved Simca with all her heart, and even though most days she wanted to clock her, she would never let anyone say a word against her. Once Paul wrote a letter to Charlie complaining about how bossy and irritating Simca could be, and Julia

made him add a footnote that this was merely his personal opinion. Still, *Volume Two* was the end of their collaboration. Late
in her life someone asked Julia her true feelings about Simone
Beck, and Julia is said to have replied, "Well, we never worked
together again, did we?"

The work that went into *Volume Two* was monumental. Julia
was no longer a Foreign Service wife with time on her hands,
but America's reigning queen of cuisine, quoted in national
magazines and invited to the White House by President Lyndon
Johnson, which led to a PBS behind-the-scenes documentary
about the White House kitchen. "The only national television
female of real authority is Julia Child," said *TV Guide* in 1968.*

Whether in Cambridge or Plascassier, Julia cooked and
wrote seven days a week, ten to twelve hours a day, for months
to make the deadline. Despite coming across as a little dotty
when she misplaced an ingredient on *The French Chef,* Julia had
become an astonishingly competent cook, a recipe-producing
machine, often with at least three dishes going at once; the chops
would be set aside to marinate while a sauce was being reduced
on the stove, while the bones and trimming of some animal or
another would be boiling in a big pot for stock, and she would
notate and amend all three recipes as she moved forward. Was
this cooking with proper love, care, and devotion? No, but it
was the mixed-bag reality of being someone with something for

---

* In a story by Marya Mannes, who also observed that as food is the domain of women, it's
not that big of a surprise.

which the world longed. After the book was completed, Julia said she would never do this kind of long encyclopedic book again, that she was tired of being locked up in the kitchen, or in her room, typing typing typing, and she wanted to cook with other people, and celebrate food with other chefs. Cooking was supposed to be fun and this was murder.

Still, their work paid off. *Mastering the Art of French Cooking, Volume Two: A Classic Continued: A New Repertory of Dishes and Techniques Carries Us into New Areas* was published in October 1970 to great acclaim. *Newsweek* thought it was even better than Volume One.

This time, Knopf ponied up for a book tour. A twenty-two-year-old publicist, newly hired, named Jane Becker,* had a thought: Why not send Julia and Simca to cities with PBS affiliates and large department stores? The store could take out a big advertisement in the newspaper announcing a demonstration by the authors of *Mastering the Art of French Cooking, Volume Two,* and the night before the event PBS could host a party for the local media. The bigwigs thought it was worth a shot, and they chose Minneapolis as the guinea pig city and set up a demonstration at Dayton's Department Store.

Jane cautioned Julia not to expect much. It seemed like a good idea, but there was also a good chance she and Simca would be making mayonnaise for a room full of empty seats.

....
* Jane Friedman, as she would soon become, went on to have a staggeringly successful publishing career, and was for many years president and CEO of HarperCollins.

They were staying at a hotel near Dayton's, and early on the morning of the demonstration, they looked out the window, and there was a line in front of the still-closed department store, snaking down the block and around the corner. Every person had in hand a copy of the new book.

Remember that being an expert doesn't mean you know everything.
In 1972, a neighbor boy, the one whose orthodontist uncle put braces on his teeth so he could get out of going to Vietnam, drove an orange Ford Ranchero with a bumper sticker that said Love Animals Don't Eat Them. I misread it every day until he moved away: Love animals don't eat *what?* I thought. I didn't know from vegetarianism. My friends' mothers may have now made vegetarian sandwiches with homemade whole wheat bread, avocados, cheese, tomatoes, and sprouts, but at our house Julia Child still ruled. My mother still cooked from *Mastering,* still stood at the stove and sautéed, deglazed, reduced, and, above all, stirred. We still ate veal scallops with mushrooms and chicken fricassee. Had Julia known, she would have been pleased, because the rest of the nation seemed to have turned against her.

The American attitude about food and cooking, which Julia had helped realize, was changing. Overnight, it seemed average citizens had become unduly preoccupied with every bite that passed their lips. Were they eating enough fruits and vegetables, enough sprouted whole grains and legumes? Were they slowly killing themselves with porterhouse steaks and baked potatoes drenched in butter? Was it possible they were harming their souls eating creatures with four legs? Was the rumor true that broccoli could think, and did that make it wrong to eat it? What about factory farms? Could you possible enjoy an omelet knowing the eggs came from a chicken housed in a poultry gulag?

Even though Julia was an early adopter—she loved her gadgets, saw no problem with the microwave, had a desktop computer as early as 1982 and a laptop shortly thereafter—she would never change her mind about eating. Food was one of life's greatest pleasures, and it should always be viewed that way. The only diet she believed in was one of moderation.

Given her insatiable curiosity and open-mindedness, her love of research and experimentation, you would think she would have been intrigued and perhaps more accepting of the new thinking about food, but the woman stood up for butter and cream as though they were her own children. She knew good and well what doctors were saying about cholesterol, and they were dead to her. She despised the idea that a cook should feel any anxiety over what her ingredients might be doing to her health. The idea of food as poison—or medicine for that matter—appalled her. She railed against the Food Police, she excoriated the Nervous Nellies, she howled at the self-imposed strictures of vegetarians. A little pâté never hurt anybody, she cried.

She was fundamentally right, of course. Decades later, people are more tortured and confused about food than ever. Where

I live in Portland, any slob can be a vegetarian.* To really get right with the food god you must be a vegan . . . who occasionally slips up and binges on maple donuts topped with bacon.

Everything that goes into our mouths has become suspect: nonfat milk, conventionally grown red delicious apples, and grapes. A single portion of Dover sole can deliver enough mercury to make you forget your own name. A store-bought cookie will kill you as sure as an automatic weapon.

On the strength of *Super Size Me*, I gave up all fast food but recently read that even a "good" burger is comprised of at least eight DNA strands, meaning eight cows went into the making of that patty, along with whatever old Band-Aids and nail trimmings found their way into the mix. As of this writing, the only food that remains pure and blameless is kale; I expect some bad news to reach us about this holiest of leafy greens any day now.

In deep middle-age, Julia spoke her mind, even when it was out-of-step with the times, even when she was wrong. How different from the young woman newly enrolled in Le Cordon Bleu, all those years ago, who said, "Being the only woman I am being careful to sit back a bit, but am being very cold-blooded indeed in a quiet way."

Over the years she would be forced to modify her position in her cookbooks and TV shows—times were changing

---

* On my Facebook newsfeed some "friend" started a long thread about some food fetish—vegetarian locavorism or something—and I quipped, "I'm an Eat-What's-Put-in-Front-of-Me-ian," and she shot back in a second, "You're what's wrong with the world."

and she knew if she was to remain relevant she had to keep up with them—but she would never fully capitulate; at the age of eighty-eight, in a radio interview, she disparaged "nutrition-type people," and told the story of one nutrition-type person who insisted that vegetables should be cooked in the least amount of water possible. "Her beans were not only gray and lifeless," said Julia, "she also died rather early."

I often wonder if some part of her demanded that she refuse to alter her position because of the fate that befell Paul, who was diagnosed with arteriosclerosis. In 1974 he underwent coronary bypass surgery; several arteries were blocked, and the procedure was then in its infancy. When he came out of surgery he seemed to be fine, but over the weeks and months it became clear that something else had gone wrong. His thoughts were a mishmash. The letter he used to whip off to his brother Charlie every evening took him days to compose. His doctors thought that perhaps he had suffered a small stroke or two while he was under anesthesia. In any case, Julia noticed that the light had gone out of him. In a cruel twist his perfect French, which had helped define him in Julia's eyes as a sophisticated man of elegance and worldliness, had completely deserted him. Now, he spoke not a word.

Of Julia's many stellar qualities—her optimism, stamina, determination, and loyalty—living with tortured ambivalence was not one of them. To allow that food she fed her beloved— the gallons of mayonnaise; beurre blanc and béarnaise sauce; the pounds of richly marbled beef and lardons; the pâtés, terrines, and foie gras; the Tarte Tatins and crème brûlée—had anything to do with his disease would be unthinkable. She loved him more than cooking, more than her life. How could butter be bad, when it had brought them so much joy?

Rule No. 10:

Every Woman Should Have a Blowtorch*

⚜

"Make every meal an occasion" sounds to me like "Live each day as though it were your last"—just plain overwrought. People do preach it, but does anyone practice? Not me! But to love your art as well as your audience does seem to make for pretty good living, day by pleasant day.

After the publication of *Mastering, Volume Two,* Julia and Simca went their separate ways. Julia would always consider her to be her French sister, but she found she could no longer abide

---

* Often attributed to Julia; actually, one of her guests said it, and she thought it was a fine idea.

the basic Dogmatic Meatballery of French cuisine. Even though she was against food fads of every stripe, the French were simply too hidebound, too fond of their rules, which Julia was against perhaps even more than she was against vegetarians. She would go on to write a dozen more good, often great, cookbooks, including *The Way to Cook,* my favorite, and the one in which she finally perfects her recipe for Tarte Tatin.

In 1980 Julia signed on to do a regular spot on ABC's morning show, *Good Morning, America.* She'd always viewed herself first and foremost as a teacher, and her cookbooks as textbooks rather than a mere extension of her brand.* After the success of *The French Chef,* the networks came courting with splashy deals and big promises, but she turned them all down, believing she belonged "with the educators" on educational TV. But PBS, the nonprofit that had become the umbrella for the country's individual educational stations, mishandled the distribution of her recent cooking series, *Julia Child & More Company,* and she was furious. Somehow, the New York affiliate, as well as a few other big stations, had failed to schedule it, and Knopf had paid a fortune for the companion guide. Julia knew that the show was essential to publicize the book, but if no one saw the show, how would they know about the book, and the whole thing was a big mess. It's possible the people at the affiliates had had enough of Julia Child, who though famous, was also sixty-eight years old. Even if ageism was not in play (doubtful), there was also

---

* A word not yet in use, but that's how she thought of it.

the matter of her association with traditional French cuisine, which, with its heavy foundation sauces and fussy insistence of wrapping in pastry dough every animal that flew, swam, or ran, had gone out of style. They didn't see that she had evolved, was evolving, and had developed her own excellent recipes for paella and pasta primavera.*

But it was a new day. Now, there were young chefs in her home state like Michael McCarty who opened Michael's in 1979 in Santa Monica, and the Austrian émigré Wolfgang Puck, chef-owner of Spago, who were cooking something called California cuisine. Alice Waters was out West too, at Chez Panisse in Berkeley, making good food that barely needed anything done to it, and her protégé, Jeremiah Tower, who asked Waters for a job in 1972 after having eaten one of her berry tarts, and would go on to open Stars in San Francisco, serving up both New American cuisine and that new type of celebrity: the chef.

Kathy and I were in film school at USC in the early 1980s. In the morning, in our apartment in the Wilshire district, before leaving for class, we would sit around drinking coffee out of chipped mugs and reading the paper and watching Julia on *Good Morning America*. We were young and mean, and we snickered at how earnest she was, and yes, how old.

Old, but entertaining. We'd be late to class before we'd miss a segment.

---

* Julia never liked pasta and didn't see what all the fuss was about.

C'EST L'ÂGE

It really does make a difference to say it in French. Are your knees starting to go, as Julia's did? *C'est l'âge!* Is your husband falling asleep in the middle of a lively and festive dinner, as Paul did during numerous occasions throughout the 1980s, requiring the person sitting next to him to give him a hard kick under the table? *C'est l'âge!*

Into her seventies Julia kept the same insane hours she always did, up by six and to bed no earlier than midnight. The rigors of taping a TV show—twelve-hour days of organized chaos—energized her. Often, when the day wrapped at 10:00 p.m., she would ask the crew where they were going to go eat dinner. Even the twenty-five-year-olds would groan with fatigue. When she wasn't taping a show, she was writing the companion book, doing her job as food editor of *Parade* magazine, traveling around the country speaking on behalf of the various causes she supported* or the American Institute of Food and Wine—a nonprofit she cofounded in 1981 with vintners Robert Mondavi and Richard Graff to promote and celebrate gastronomy in America—guest lecturing at a cooking school, or attending a ceremony to collect one of the many honorary doctorates† she was snapping up like paperbacks at a yard sale.

---

* Like Planned Parenthood, which was as controversial then as now. Once she caused a stir by noting that if women had easy access to more birth control there'd be less abortions.

† She received honorary degrees from Brown, Harvard, Boston University, Smith (Ha!), Rutgers, Johnson and Wales University, The Culinary Institute of America at Hyde Park, Newberry College, and the California State University.

In addition, most nights she hosted an informal dinner party at the big gray clapboard house on Irving Street in Cambridge. Julia never prepared dinner ahead. If she invited you, you were expected to pitch in. On any given night John Kenneth Galbraith—esteemed economist, author, Harvard professor, and President Kennedy's ambassador to India—could be seen at the sink peeling carrots, or international chef Jacques Pépin, setting out the pâté, or celebrated English cookbook author Jane Grigson, peeling potatoes. Every chef who came to Boston wound up at Julia's table. You always ate in the kitchen, and her hors d'oeuvres were always the same: Pepperidge Farm Goldfish.

She attributed her vim and stamina to being made of "good pioneer stock," and aside from her knees, which were chronically inflamed and sometimes caused her to sob with pain at the end of the day, she really was a miracle of fine health.

But the same could not be said of Paul. He recovered somewhat from his stroke, and he was able to get back to his painting and photography, but his personality had become less complex; he'd become dull-witted and confused. Still, Julia kept him as her constant companion. When she was on the set doing a show, he was given the role of Official Photographer, but there was always another photographer on hand to make sure everything was done right. At the beginning of what would be diagnosed as dementia, he would blurt out whatever he was thinking at inopportune moments. "Yes, Paul," Julia would say, as though it were the most normal thing, which it was. Paul behaving oddly had become the new normal. *C'est l'âge.*

The sudden death of his twin, Charlie, in 1983, was a setback from which he never recovered, and in 1988 he walked out of their house in Cambridge, hopped in a cab idling at the curb, and drove away to he knew not where. For Julia, that was the sign she could no longer care for him, and the next year she settled him in a nursing home where, until the day he died in 1994, she visited or called him every day.

When Simca died in 1991 at the age of eighty-seven, Julia turned over the keys to La Pitchoune to Simca's family, according to the agreement she and Paul had made with her nearly thirty years before. As much as Julia loved the places of her life, she loved the people more. Now that Simca and her husband, Jean, were gone, now that Jim Beard, who "slid off the raft" in 1985, wouldn't be coming to visit, and Paul was too weak to travel, Provence was no longer the same. The fields of wild lavender were being bulldozed to make way for new houses, and people no longer shopped at their local butchers, bakers, and cheese makers, but at the supermarket. She was appalled to realize it reminded her of the worst of Southern California.

Julia spent one last summer in Provence with her sister, Dort, who brought her children, Julia's nieces and nephews. Julia set her alarm at 2:00 a.m. to call Paul every day back in Cambridge. Even though they were separated by an ocean, they were still Pulia. She played golf, tidied up, and cooked. Julia Child was not the sentimental sort. When she was done with something, she was done. She ate a final meal of *Boeuf en Daube à la Provençal*—French pot roast—then closed up La Peetch and moved back to California, where she lived for another busy decade. She didn't just *have* a blowtorch, she was a blowtorch.

Old age. I don't know when it really starts, and I'm not interested in finding out. Julia pretty much ignored the whole thing, and that may be the only real lesson there is for the end of our days. Just pretend like it isn't happening, until you have no choice but to accept reality. If you're lucky, like Julia, you'll die peacefully in your sleep after having enjoyed a dinner of onion soup.

Love the young.

Julia, by nature, was always interested in what was around the next bend. Her disinclination to dwell on the past was probably some kind of psychological disorder. Professionally, she was always curious about what the next crop of chefs were up to, even if she didn't agree with them. All those young master chefs mentioned earlier? They all became friends; some were featured on *In Julia's Kitchen with Master Chefs*, where she flew around the world, visiting each chef in his or her own kitchen.

Thus, with every new television series, or whenever she took on a project that required help, a squad of eager young'uns—production assistants, prep cooks, associate producers—entered her life and most often became friends. They were Tina, Stephanie, Suzy; they were Liz, Sara, and Jocelyn. They were full of energy, hardworking, and when the show, magazine editorship, class, or demonstration was finished and Julia took a group photo with them, she instructed them to say not cheese, but *souf-flé*, to get the proper slightly opened mouth smile, and they would. In the picture they would look like a bunch of friends in white aprons, and in most cases that's what they were. Julia didn't look like anyone's grandmother, or even anyone's mother.

In Jewish tradition, if a funeral procession meets a wedding procession at a crossroads, the wedding procession is given right-of-way. Once you reach a certain age you basically have two choices: You can be the neighbor who yells "Get off my lawn!" and grouses about kids today, or you can let the wedding procession pass. Or, you can do as Julia did, and leave the funeral procession and *join* the wedding procession.

On August 15, 1992, Julia turned eighty, and the nation was in the mood to celebrate her. Fame is mysterious. What was so special about her eightieth birthday? Is not seventy-five a bigger milestone? Is not living to ninety a more staggering achievement?

Had it been up to Julia, she would have ignored the day completely, but then she agreed to attend a few birthday benefits for the American Institute of Food and Wine, which she helped found, and soon, anyone who could wangle a few chefs and rent a hotel banquet room wanted to hold a party for Julia, *La Dame du Siècle*, who had taught America how to cook.

It mattered not that French cooking was passé, that now fine dining was all Asian fusion, "architectural" presentation, prosciutto-wrapped figs, mango/jicama slaw, sundried tomatoes, barley risotto, blackened fish and pork and tomatillo chili, and that home cooks had discovered "lite" dairy products, boneless skinless chicken breasts, and I Can't Believe It's Not Butter. The parties, which began months before Julia's birthday, continued into 1993. In New Orleans and San Francisco, in Las Vegas, Miami, and Napa, glasses were raised, toasts were made, sumptuous feasts were prepared and consumed.

In New York City three hundred guests showed up at The Rainbow Room and paid $200 each to enjoy a multicourse meal prepared by fourteen chefs. Julia was presented with a four-foot whisk enrobed in pearls. She tossed it over her shoulder, baseball bat–style, and marched around the room. WGBH in Boston threw her a party at the Copley Plaza Hotel, and the Boston Pops played "Fanfare with Pots and Pans" on whisks, pots, and pans. Diana Rigg stood and read a poem written by Paul decades earlier about Julia's cooking prowess, and Julia sat there and cried. In Southern California, at the Ritz Carlton in Marina del Rey, nine of France's top Michelin star chefs were flown in to collaborate on a $350 a plate feast, assisted by forty-four of the best American French chefs and twenty sous chefs. Before the dinner, sixty different kinds of hors d'oeuvres were passed* At the Washington, D.C., bash† the finale consisted of three cakes it had taken the pastry chefs three months to construct.

---

* Not one of them was Pepperidge Farm Goldfish.

† Picketed by vegetarians who carried signs that said ANIMALS BEWARE! JULIA IS HUNGRY! Even though she had publicly apologized in 1987 for anything she might have said to insult them, they remained incensed at her treatment of animals.

There were smaller parties, too. Jasper White held a private party at his restaurant in Cambridge, and Pam Fiore, editor of *Travel + Leisure,* hosted a dinner at her New York apartment, where the guests regaled Julia with songs Fiore had penned especially for the occasion, including one called "What Child Is This?"

Julia, who even at eighty had the stamina of a sled dog at peak training, attended all three hundred of them.

Enjoy the power of man power.
Nancy Verde Barr was one of Julia's young friends. A good twenty years younger and a full foot shorter than Julia, Verde Barr was a graduate of Madeleine Kamman's Modern Gourmet cooking school and owned a school of her own. Kamman, born in Paris and educated at the Sorbonne, was a *Super-Française* and would snort with derision at the mere mention of Julia's name, who she dismissed as a mere TV cook, and not a real chef. But Julia didn't hold this against Nancy, with whom she traveled and hung out for the last twenty or so years of her life.

By the early 1990s, Julia lived alone, visiting Paul every day when she was in town, but taking Nancy as her escort to the many dinners, receptions, lectures, benefits, and parties (including most of those birthday parties) to which she was invited. One day she told Nancy that they should really make a point of finding some nice men, because wasn't life just that much more fun with men around? Nancy, perhaps to humor her, agreed, but said nice men weren't that easy to find.

Less than a week later, Julia called Nancy and said not to worry about her, that she'd found a man. John McJennett was an old friend of Paul's. When Paul had lived in Paris in the 1920s, he'd crashed the twenty-first birthday party of McJennett's late wife. They'd stayed friends throughout the years, and now he and Julia were smitten. McJennett was a he-man, a Harvard man, Marine, and semiprofessional baseball player who was an inch taller than Julia (!) and knew nothing about cuisine.

He squired her around for years and sometimes dropped hints about getting married, forgetting that Julia was married. She confided in Nancy about his proposals, mock-groaning that she already had taken care of one old man, and she didn't need another one! Did she love him? Who knows. She loved the old mold that he came from, that straight-up manly man, simple as the steak and baked potato he preferred. Perhaps he reminded her of Pop, only nicer, but he enlivened her days.

On May 12, 1994, Julia and John were having a late dinner at Jasper's, after a long day of filming *Master Chefs*, when word came that Paul had died. Julia bolted up from the table and raced to the nursing home to see for herself. Three days later a wisteria Paul had planted in the yard decades earlier bloomed for the first time. Even though he had been sick for so long, Julia cried for days.

Julia Wish

James Thurber, humorist and dog person, said, "Man is troubled by what might be called the Dog Wish, a strange and involved compulsion to be as happy and carefree as a dog." Those of us who admire Julia are troubled by the wish to be as happy and carefree as she, who had no fear, didn't worry, didn't fret, and sobbed herself sick when she was grief-stricken, then when her tears were dry, moved on to the next thing.

As Julia explains for us in *Julia Child & Company* (1978), French cuisine is not only haute cuisine, fine dining at one of those four-star restaurants with exotic ingredients* and no prices on the menu. The French have an itch to classify every-thing they encounter, and their famous cooking is no excep-tion. In its time, people supposed *Mastering the Art of French Cooking* was instructing Americans on how to make haute cui-sine, but it was actually proffering recipes from *la cuisine bour-geoise,* one step down from haute cuisine.† One step down from that is *la cuisine de famille,* which Julia typifies as a Sunday lunch with a starter of sliced tomatoes vinaigrette, followed by a roast leg of lamb with green beans, then the cheese course, followed by a nice apple tart. One step below that is what is referred to as peasant cooking or *la cuisine bonne femme*: a hardy soup, big pieces of crusty bread, followed by a piece of fruit for dessert. Late last century nouvelle cuisine came along (three spears of asparagus arranged artfully on a plate), then *cuisine minceur,* literally "slimming cooking" (two spears

---

* Truffles, they always have truffles.

† However gifted, no mere mortal can make haute cuisine, you must be a classically trained chef.

of asparagus arranged artfully on a plate). It goes without saying that there is no name for a cuisine that includes standing
in the middle of the kitchen eating a hot dog you've cooked
over the burner.

Missing from this list is *la cuisine Julia,* the foundation of
everything we cook today. *La cuisine Julia* is not French, but
Frenchy. Its founding philosophy is liberal rather than classical,
believing that there is always room for variation, experimentation,
and completely screwing up. Fresh ingredients are preferred, but
no one is sent to food hell for opening a can of cream of mushroom soup. *La cuisine Julia* is, above all, serious; it renounces
shortcuts, sloppiness, or a lack of attention to details. It must be
performed with time and love, and a little imperfection.

Not long ago a woman who grew up on my street in Whittier
contacted me and said she was going through some old books
at her parents' house and came across a cookbook published in
1966 by Las Damas, a women's club my mother belonged to.
She saw my mother had contributed to it and wondered if I'd
be interested in having it. *Oh, man!* I thought, in the exact voice
of the girl I was when my mother was making all those recipes.

The cookbook is the size of a hardback book and comb-
bound with a brown plastic comb. It is dedicated to "The Modern Home. In our Home today, and always, Life is Centered
around Our Kitchens."

The recipes are what you would expect from a suburban 1960s cookbook: lots of casseroles, lots of recipes with "easy" in the title, terse instructions, practically haikus: "Brown meat. Add remaining ingredients. Serve over Fritos."

My mother contributed recipes for Nuts 'n Bolts ("Hors d'Oeuvres, Party and T.V. Snacks"), Baked Chicken Breasts (which she recommends serving with Rice Pilaf and Caesar Salad), Chafing Dish Gourmet (the less said about this the better), Mixed Vegetables Mornay (using a box of Birds Eye Frozen Mixed Vegetables), and Beef Stroganoff.

The stroganoff instructions are the longest in the book, and at the end, my mother thought to include this: "Note: Dill greatly enhances the flavor of meat, potatoes, and vegetables. Each year I buy a bunch of dill and preserve it by cutting off the sprigs, discarding the stalks, and packing in salt in a large jar, which I keep in the refrigerator. When ready to use, simply wash a sprig in cold water."

Instantly, I recognized the internalized voice of Julia, informing, guiding, and reassuring.

I wish I could say that I was inspired to make my mother's beef stroganoff that very night, and that it was so delicious my complicated feelings about food and cooking were transformed forever, as were Julia's on that long ago day in Rouen, but *beef stroganoff?*

Still, there is hope for me yet. Remember the fish filets poached in white wine that Kathy and I almost didn't make that day in Paris? We did not give up that night. Instead, we opened a bottle of our three-euro Chardonnay and stumbled forward, poaching the filets in our makeshift white wine and vegetable broth, covering it with buttered notebook paper to hold in the heat, and continuing to simmer it on top of the stove, because we had no oven. It was in all ways wrong, but we proceeded as if we were following Julia's recipe to the letter.

While Kathy was monitoring the fish, I assembled the egg yolk sauce, for that is the homely anglicized name of *Sauce à la Parisienne,* making a roux from the fish poaching stock, flour, and that stupendous French butter, then adding the cream and yolks. It was not as flavorful as *Sauce Hollandaise* but much sturdier and more difficult to ruin, and it could be made without a whisk.

We sautéed some beautiful, slender haricots verts and shallots, threw together a green salad, grabbed a baguette, and sat down at our table in front of the window looking out on the Romanian Embassy. Next door, we could hear our neighbor yelling. We poured more wine, toasted our ability to persevere, and dug in.

Reader, it was perfectly delicious.

A Reading List

These were the titles I read and reread as I thought and wrote about the woman we came to know simply as Julia. A complete list of Julia Child's books, television shows, and DVDs can be found at www.juliachild foundation.org.

JULIA CHILD

Appetite for Life: The Biography of Julia Child by Noël Riley Fitch

As Always, Julia: The Letters of Julia Child & Avis DeVoto, edited by Joan Reardon

Backstage with Julia: My Years with Julia Child by Nancy Verde Barr

A Covert Affair: Julia Child and Paul Child in the OSS by Jennet Conant

Dearie: The Remarkable Life of Julia Child by Bob Spitz

Julia Child: A Life by Laura Shapiro

Julia Child's The French Chef by Dana Polan

M.F.K. Fisher, Julia Child & Alice Waters: Celebrating the Pleasures of the Table by Joan Reardon

My Life in France by Julia Child and Alex Prud'homme

Sisterhood of Spies: The Women of the OSS by Elizabeth P. McIntosh

AND OTHERS

The Art of Eating: 50th Anniversary Edition by M.F.K. Fisher

Heat: An Amateur's Adventures as Kitchen Slave, Line Cook, Pasta-Maker, and Apprentice to a Dante-Quoting Butcher in Tuscany by Bill Buford

The I Hate to Cook Book by Peg Bracken

Julie & Julia: 365 Days, 524 Recipes, 1 Tiny Apartment Kitchen by Julie Powell

My Kitchen Wars by Betty Fussell
Paris Journal 1944–1955 by Janet Flanner
The Physiology of Taste: Or Meditations on Transcendental Gastronomy by
Jean Anthelme Brillat-Savarin
The Tenth Muse: My Life in Food by Judith Jones

GENERAL FOOD HISTORY

The Omnivore's Dilemma: A Natural History of Four Meals by Michael
Pollan
Setting the Table for Julia Child: Gourmet Dining in America, 1934–1961
by David Strauss
Something from the Oven: Reinventing Dinner in 1950s America by Laura
Shapiro
The United States of Arugula: How We Became a Gourmet Nation by David
Kamp
Watching What We Eat: The Evolution of Television Cooking Shows by
Kathleen Collins

Acknowledgments

I was reminded recently of the old German proverb, "To start is easy, to persist an art." People who have practiced the art of persisting with me, throughout the writing of this book, and to whom I owe a debt of gratitude:

Editor extraordinaire Lara Asher at Globe Pequot Press, for saying a big yes to Julia. Also, her top-notch crew: Lauren Brancato, Shana Capozza, Jessica DeFranco, Meredith Dias, Janice Goldklang, Kate Hertzog, and Ann Seifert. At Inkwell Management: David Forrer, Nathaniel Jacks, Richard Pine, Hannah Schwartz, and Kim Witherspoon, without whom . . . well, they know.

Others who offered insight, wisdom, and support, sometimes all three: Elizabeth Benedict, Leslie Bilderback, Kathy Budas, Lynne Bollinger Christensen, Hannah Concannon, Marcelline Dormont, Kim Dower, Debbie Guyol, Deb Nies, Randy Rollison, Danna Schaeffer, Lisa Spiegel, Abby Bliss White.

A special *merci beaucoup* to Kathie Alex for sharing La Pitchoune with me.

To Jerrod Allen and Fiona Baker: Paul said it best, about Julia: You are the butter to my bread, you are the breath to my life.

Notes
....

Abbreviations of names cited in the notes:
ADV: Avis DeVoto
CMW: Carolyn "Caro" McWilliams
DdS: Dorothy de Santillana
GK: George Kubler
JC: Julia Child
PC: Paul Child
SB: Simone Beck

RULE #1: LIVE WITH ABANDON

13. *"I've finally found . . ."* JC to ADV, 1952, Schlesinger Library, Radcliffe Center for Advance Study at Harvard University.

RULE #2: PLAY THE EMPEROR

25. *"I'm all for . . ."* Mike Sager, "Julia Child: What I've Learned," *Esquire*, June 2001.
42. *"At last, I . . ."* Julia Child, Alex Prud'homme, *My Life in France* (New York: Knopf, 2006), 112.
42. *"felt like a frump . . ."* JC to ADV, 1953, Schlesinger Library.

RULE #3: LEARN TO BE AMUSED

47. *"One's best evenings . . ."* JC to ADV, 1953, Schlesinger Library.
50. *". . .with the design . . ."* Will of Sophia Smith, 1870, www.smith.edu.
52. *"I only wish . . ."* JC to CMW, Noël Riley Fitch, *Appetite for Life: The Biography of Julia Child* (New York: Doubleday, 1997), 63.

52. *"Passing tests doesn't . . ."* Noam Chomsky, *The Purpose of Education,* Learning Without Frontiers Conference, January 25, 2012.
56. *"All I want . . ."* Bob Spitz, *Dearie: The Remarkable Life of Julia Child* (New York: Knopf, 2012), 85–86.
58. *"I am quite . . ." Appetite for Life,* 77.

RULE #4: OBEY YOUR WHIMS

76. *"She also had . . ."* Joan Juliet Buck, "Joan Juliet Buck on Being in Awe of Nora Ephron," *The Daily Beast,* June 27, 2012.
78. *"I was a member . . ."* Bill Buford, *Heat: An Amateur's Adventures as Kitchen Slave, Line Cook, Pasta-Maker, and Apprentice to a Dante-Quoting Butcher in Tuscany* (New York: Knopf, 2006), 20.
80. *"I do love . . ."* Jennet Conant, *A Covert Affair: Julia Child and Paul Child in the OSS* (New York: Simon & Schuster, 2011), 224.
84. *"He is an intellectual . . ."* JC to ADV, March 1953, Schlesinger Library.
86. *"cataloging and channeling . . ."* Greg Miller, "Files from WWll Office of Strategic Services Are Secret No More," *Los Angeles Times,* August 15, 2008.

RULE #5: ALL YOU NEED IS A KITCHEN AND A BEDROOM

89. *"We analyzed one . . ."* Julia Child, Alex Prud'homme, *My Life in France* (New York: Knopf, 2006), 25.
95. *"How magnificent to . . ."* Ibid., 68.
96. *"Theoretically a good . . ."* Julia Child, Louisette Bertholle, Simone Beck, *Mastering the Art of French Cooking, Vol. 1* (New York: Knopf, 1983) (Updated edition), 3.
99. *"bring out the best . . ."* PC to GK, 1949, Schlesinger Library.
108. *"The Puritans turned . . ."* Tim Kreider, "The Busy Trap," *New York Times,* June 30, 2012.
109 *"If we could . . ."* Ruth Reichl, "Julia Child's Recipe for a Thoroughly Modern Marriage," *Smithsonian,* June 2012.
112. *"except for La Cuisine . . ."* JC to ADV, 1953, Schlesinger Library.

Rule #6: To Be Happy, Work Hard

117. "*There is so much . . .*" JC to ADV, April 1953, Schlesinger Library.
121. "*a perfectly . . .*" ADV to JC, 1953, Joan Reardon, ed., *As Always, Julia: The Letters of Julia Child & Avis DeVoto* (New York: Houghton Mifflin Harcourt, 2010), 29.
121. "*This is a . . .*" Julia Child, Louisette Bertholle, Simone Beck, *Mastering the Art of French Cooking, Vol. 1* (New York: Knopf, 1983) (Updated edition), xxx.
124. "*We also ran . . .*" JC to ADV, 1953, Schlesinger Library.
126. "*. . . a nice photo . . .*" JC to ADV, 1953, Schlesinger Library.
133. "*. . . distressing examples of . . .*" JC to ADV, 1953, Schlesinger Library.

Rule #7: Solve the Problem in Front of You

139. "*If you get . . .*" Polly Frost, "Julia Child," *Interview*, August 1989.
143. "*the one activity . . .*" Betty Fussell, *My Kitchen Wars: A Memoir* (New York, North Point Press, 1999), 152.
143. "*This was no . . .*" Ibid., 155.
147. "*old black honey . . .*" M.F.K. Fisher, *The Art of Eating: 50th Anniversary Edition* (Hoboken: Wiley Publishing, Inc., 2004), 81.
147. "*for a painfully . . .*" Ibid., 81.
147. "*go ahead as so many . . .*" Laura Shapiro, *Julia Child: A Life* (New York: Viking Penguin, 2007), 83.
148. "*We intend to . . .*" JC to ADV, 1958, Schlesinger Library.
149. "*. . . short and snappy . . .*" JC to DdS, 1958, Joan Reardon, ed., *As Always, Julia: The Letters of Julia Child & Avis DeVoto* (New York: Houghton Mifflin Harcourt, 2010), 259.
149. "*unusual vegetable dishes . . .*" JC to DdS, 1958, *As Always, Julia*, 259.
155. "*I have a . . .*" ADV to JC, 1955, ibid., 221.
155. "*Use finesse as . . .*" ADV to JC, 1953, ibid., 79.
155. "*triumph of Norwegian . . .*" JC to ADV, 1959, Schlesinger Library.
156. "*Dearest Simca and . . .*" JC to SB and ADV, 1959, Schlesinger Library.

Rule #8: Cooking Means Never Saying You're Sorry

160. *"Probably the most . . ."* Craig Claiborne, "Glorious Recipes; Art of French Cooking Does Not Concede to U.S. Tastes. Text Is Simply Written for Persons Who Enjoy Cuisine," *New York Times*, October 18, 1961.

164. *"the talk of . . ."* Laura Shapiro, *Julia Child: A Life* (New York: Viking Penguin, 2007), 110.

166. *"We're doing making . . ."* Julia Child, "Your Own French Onion Soup," *The French Chef.* WGBH, Boston. Season 1, 1963.

166. *"cut your hand . . ."* Ibid.

166. *"The knife is . . ."* Ibid.

166. *"Knives are your . . ."* Ibid.

167. *"If you're serious . . ."* Ibid.

167. *"you'll enjoy it . . ."* Ibid.

167. *"You'll notice I . . ."* Ibid.

167. *"Look at this!"* Ibid.

167. *"They're perfectly delicious . . ."* Ibid.

167. *"It looks awful . . ."* Ibid.

168. *"It's so hot . . ."* Ibid.

168. *"It's possibly browned . . ."* Ibid.

168. *"California Mountain Red"* Ibid.

168. *"When you've added . . ."* Ibid.

170. *"vile eggs Florentine . . ."* Julia Child, Alex Prud'homme, *My Life in France* (New York: Knopf, 2006), 90.

173. *"These are the . . ."* "To Roast a Chicken," *The French Chef.* WGBH, Boston. Season 1, 1963.

174. *"This chicken is . . ."* Ibid.

174. *"This chicken weighs. . ."* Ibid.

174. *"It's twice as . . ."* Ibid.

178. *"Stop gasping"* . . . *"Wipe brow"* Marilyn Mellowes, "About Julia Child," *American Masters,* June 2005.

Rule #9: Make the World Your Oyster (Stew)

187. "*The lady with . . .*" Christina Crapanzano, "The 25 Most Powerful Women of the Last Century," *Time,* Nov. 18, 2010.

188. "*the definition of . . .*" Tina Fey, *Bossypants* (New York: Reagan Arthur Books, 2011), 271.

191. "*I learned the . . .*" Janis Ian, "At Seventeen," *Between the Lines,* Columbia Records, August 1975.

194. "*Left breast off*" Noël Riley Fitch, *Appetite for Life: The Biography of Julia Child* (New York: Doubleday, 1997), 336.

196. "*It was like . . .*" Julia Child, Simone Beck. *Mastering the Art of French Cooking, Vol. 2: A Classic Continued: A New Repertory of Dishes and Techniques Carries Us into New Areas* (New York: Alfred A. Knopf, 1970), x.

201. "*The only national . . .*" Marya Mannes, *TV Guide,* 1968 [clipping].

205. "*Being the only . . .*" Laura Shapiro, *Julia Child: A Life* (New York: Viking Penguin, 2007), 33.

206. "*Her beans were . . .*" JC, interview with Evan Kleiman, *Good Food,* KCRW, Santa Monica, 2000.

Rule #10: Every Woman Should Have a Blowtorch

209. "*Make every meal . . .*" Julia Child, *Julia Child & Company* (New York: Alfred A. Knopf, 1978), 50.

219. "*Man is troubled . . .*" James Thurber, *The Dog Department: James Thurber on Hounds, Scotties, and Talking Poodles* (New York: Harper, 2001), 114.

222. "*Note: Dill greatly . . .*" *Las Damas Cook Book* (Kansas City: North American Press, 1966), 47.

About the Author

Karen Karbo's first novel, *Trespassers Welcome Here,* was a *New York Times* Notable Book of the Year and a Village Voice Top Ten Book of the Year. Her other two adult novels, *The Diamond Lane* and *Motherhood Made a Man Out of Me,* were also named NYT Notable Books. Her 2004 memoir, *The Stuff of Life,* about the last year she spent with her father before his death, was a NYT Notable Book, a *People* Magazine Critics' Choice, a Books for a Better Life Award finalist, and a winner of the Oregon Book Award for Creative Nonfiction. Her short stories, essays, articles, and reviews have appeared in *Elle, Vogue, Esquire, Outside,* the *New York Times,* Salon.com, and other magazines. She is a recipient of a National Endowment for the Arts Fellowship in Fiction and a winner of the General Electric Younger Writer Award.

Karbo is most well known for her best-selling Kick Ass Women series, which includes *How Georgia Became O'Keeffe,* the bestseller *The Gospel According to Coco Chanel,* and *How to Hepburn.* Karen grew up in Los Angeles, California, and lives in Portland, Oregon, where she continues to kick ass.